'He Belonged to Us'

By

Aurora Borealis

ISBN: 1-4033-8135-6 (e-book)
ISBN: 1-4033-8136-4 (Paperback)
ISBN: 1-4033-8137-2 (RocketBook)

Library of Congress Control Number: 2002094887

This book is printed on acid free paper.

Printed in the United States of America
Bloomington, IN

1stBooks - rev. 10/11/02

THIS BOOK IS WRITTEN WITH A

'SILENT PRAYER'

PLEASE 'JESUS'

IF IT SAVES ONE YOUNG LIFE

'WE HAVE SUCCEEDED'

iv

TABLE OF CONTENTS

CHAPTER 1

THE BEAUTIFUL EARLY JULY

DAY

Aurora Borealis

What a beautiful, early July day it was; when my Son, Patrick and I were returning from shopping.

We were shopping for our upcoming vacation to Northern Michigan.

We were stopped in the left turn lane, waiting for the oncoming traffic to clear; waiting to turn into the condo development where we resided.

My nine year old son, had dropped his container of Gatorade, he asked me; "Mom, can I take my seat belt off and get my Gatorade," "Please Mom?"

I answered, "Yes, make it fast," "Get that seatbelt on as fast as possible."

"This is a very busy highway Patty."

A loud voice shouted, "Watch Out!"

Feeling another vehicle slamming into the back of ours; I turned my head and body towards My Young Son.

I outstretched my right arm and hand to stop Patrick from flying through the windshield.

Success; MY Son was safe!

I turned the vehicle into the roadway where we resided. Turning off the car; I took Patty and sat under a tree.

My Son was fine; "Thank you, 'Jesus'."

Quickly, an ambulance arrived and MY Son and I were transported to a hospital. The female of the other vehicle was in the ambulance too.

All three of us were to be examined for injuries.

The nurses called my husband at work; he arrived at the hospital.

Patrick was fine; free from injuries.

My husband was told; "She suffered a serious whiplash injury;" "this will take time for her to recover."

4

As the days went by, I realized I could not hold my head up; the pain was too intense. My eyes would not focus as they had prior to the strong impact from the accident.

I had to recover; many hours were spent going from one doctor to another. I had my beautiful young son to raise.

After months; I was referred into the 'right' neurologist and underwent many tests, physical therapy and daily medications.

I had saved Patrick's life; I was to live the rest of my days with a serious condition.

5

This condition involved damage to my neck muscles and nerves; a condition called 'Post Traumatic Spasmodic Torticollis.'

My husband tried to be supportive of me throughout the early months.

He worked long hours in a factory; when at home; he would sit back and drink one beer after another. When his daily twelve pac was gone; he was also gone; gone to bed!

He was in denial over my injuries and insisted that I carry on and do all the things I had before. I tried, as time went on; I realized I could 'no longer' hold my head in a straight centered position. Some days; the pain was so intense; I would sleep on the hard floor flat on my back.

This helped with the pain and I managed to get some sleep and rest.

Making this situation even worse was my own auto insurance company.

They would not cooperate with the payment of my medical expenses despite my coverage. Everyone wants to be paid for their work. I had 'no choice' but to hire an attorney. This turned into quite a lengthy ordeal.

Aurora Borealis

In 1994; everything fell into place with the Insurance Company. I had accepted the fact; my neck injuries were permanent. I had been given a 'cross' to carry for the rest of my life. I accept this!

I concentrated on being a wife and a Mother. My Husband was an alcoholic; I knew this. There were days when I was troubled and wondered.

Wondered; "Is this the 'right' environment to raise a young, impressionable boy?"

He loved us, however; with his drinking he began to embarrass Patrick and also me.

This was a combination of his excessive drinking and associated behavior.

I gave serious thought to leaving and moving to our summer place in Northern Michigan.

One day arriving home from work; he began his daily drinking routine and 'came right out with it.'

"How much does it take to get rid of you?"

"When can you and Patty go; and leave me alone?"

"I am not attracted to women your age;" 'I like young women."

9

"Get out of my place."

I tried not to let this mental and emotional pain show. I already lived with physical pain; he was adding even more to my load.

Alcoholism and its associated problems inflicts mental and emotional pain on others.

Shortly afterward; our daughter called.

I will never forget this day!

Patty and I were both downstairs, he was watching a movie, I was doing my stretches and exercises.

I heard him say to Our Daughter; "The best thing for this family would be;"

10

"For Your Mother to go up North and die!"

Waiting for him to leave for work the next day; I knew what had to be done for me and Patrick. I had given this a lot of thought; I called my attorney and scheduled an appointment.

I had to file for a divorce and remove myself and My Impressionable, young son from this 'drunken, cruel man and environment.'

On November 17 1994, Patty and I got into a fully loaded car.

Patty had to hold his Little Parakeet in her cage on his lap.

On his lap for the long drive to our Summer place in Northern Michigan.

I wanted Patrick to grow up away from alcohol. I also wanted him to realize that men do not treat women in this manner.

'Thinking' I had made the right decision; we began our new lives in the Northwoods of Michigan.

CHAPTER 2

OUR PLACE IN THE

NORTHWOODS

Aurora Borealis

Our place in the Northwoods was purchased as our get-a-way place from downstate. When Patrick and I arrived there in November, it was a different story than being there in the summer.

The day after our arrival, Patrick asked me if I would take him into the Village; to get some sand paper for a wooden key he had made downstate.

He wanted to finish sanding it, next stain it and hang it on the kitchen wall.

Patty was so proud of his first wood project.

I said 'alright Patty we have to go there and right back, as I think there is something wrong with the propane stove in the living room and we have to figure it out today."

Off we went into the Village. This Village appeared to be so quiet and peaceful. A Small Village with a connecting Ferry to a Larger Island.

I waited in the car as Patty went into the hardware store and came out with his sandpaper; happy he was and proud.

Not too far down the road on the way home; our car just stopped.

No matter what I did—it would not start. My son and I went to a couple of houses only to find no one answered.

15

Aurora Borealis

My son strived to be a basketball player in school, Patty was used to running.

I sat in the car waiting and he ran into the service station in the Village.

To my surprise he arrived back real fast; riding in a tow truck with the younger man who worked at the service station.

No go—the car would not start—it was the timing chain.

Next step—we rode in the tow truck into the Service Station.

The Younger man gave us a ride home—it was going to take some time to get our car back. Our car was a foreign make.

In the early afternoon, that exact day, the wind started to blow strong. As each hour went by the wind blew stronger and stronger. The power went out and remained out for three days. It was getting colder inside.

I had called a heating repair man from the Village; he did not come out or call back.

I thought what are we going to do; we went to a neighbors, Patrick and I met over the summer. We got lucky on this; he came down and between Patrick and him; the propane stove in the living room worked once again. We had some heat, as it operated also without electricity.

Next problem; we could not get anywhere to get food and supplies.

Our place was located miles away from the Village and many, many miles away from a town of any size.

I noticed the older man who sold us our summer place was at his cabin.

I went over and told him about the car and he agreed to take me and Patrick into a distant neighboring Community; the next day for what we needed.

We went shopping for food and supplies.

Three, kind men from the small inland lake area where we resided—helped Patrick and me.

A wonderful woman friend down the street drove me and Patty into the Village to get him enrolled in school. I love her for being a real true friend; always there when you need help in anyway.

Patrick went to school; the storm stopped; the car was repaired and I began to tighten up and winterize a summer place. Our first two winters were incredibly hard.

We lived on a small weekly income— alimony and child support. I could not work; I was disabled from my auto accident.

Between the propane and electric bills; I had to be really creative with my cooking.

19

Aurora Borealis

Patrick and I never went hungry—sometimes we came close.

Along with all the hardships; we had lots of fun together.

Harsh winter storms would blow in and dump many feet of snow on us; we did not have a snowthrower yet—only shovels. Patty and I would fuel up on food; bundle up; go outside and shovel, talk and laugh. In we would go again; to fuel up on food ; out we would go again.

Eventually Patrick took over all the snow removal work. A few times each winter he would get up on the roofs and clear them off;

20

he would do this also for seasonal people who contacted him.

Patty and I watched many movies together; played card games and other games. Mother and Son: through the Good Times and the Hard Times.

Patty and I did these things—and found many treasured moments.

It was hard to do other things as we did not have the money. We had started Orthodontic Work on Patrick's teeth downstate, we had to squeeze this into the budget too. The winter drives back and forth into the orthodontist's office were at times scary, dangerous driving. We even managed to buy sporting cards to continue our collection we were building. Between My Son and I, and our combined knowledge of Country Music and Sports Trivia, we won many prizes and awaited the arrival of the mailman. We found great joy and happiness at this time in those things in life that do not require lots of money.

In the Spring Patrick would rake the yard—a large yard—I would help out as well as I could. We planted flowers and vegetables together . The yardwork was done as a team. I bought Patrick an old smaller riding lawn mower and a weed-whacker. Together our yard always looked beautiful.

Patty and I would ride our bikes down to the little shoreline of the inland lake and swim together. We both loved to fish and spent many happy hours, fishing off of the neighbor's dock or driving to other locations to fish.

In My Heart—I sensed my son was greatly happy. I saw happiness and joy radiating from his smiling young face. A shortage of money did not seem to bother him. Patty was happy and this in return made me a very happy Mother too.

CHAPTER 3

PATRICK'S LOVE OF BALLS

Patty; from a little baby boy loved balls. His love of balls quickly turned into a love for the game of basketball. He played basketball during the 7th and 8th grades of school in this Village. Patrick would practice every chance he got; during one of the years of school; he wanted a large piece of plywood for a backboard, a basketball hoop and net. This was all he wanted from me for his birthday; well, also a birthday party with some of his school friends at the house for a sleep-over.

An old high school friend of mine came out to our place; together, he and Patty installed the backboard, hoop and net on an outer building in the yard. Next we put in concrete

25

stepping stones and concrete for a smooth dribbling surface. This is where Patrick practiced basketball shots and dribbling over and over again; throughout all his basketball playing years for this small rural school. In the garage; He created another basketball area; where he would practice on snowy or rainy days.

Patty, with the love and patience of a neighbor learned how to use a compound bow and arrow. Another birthday present he wanted, was more wood and a thick Styrofoam target; he placed this out in the back of the house where he practiced archery. He took a hunting class, got a license and each day after school; he would spend his time sitting in one of his blinds waiting for a "Buck" to come in.

That day came; and with one bent crooked arrow; he downed his first Buck. My son excitedly came into the house; in a real hurry.

"Mom I got one, I have to change real fast and track it down before it gets too dark."

Patty did exactly that and with the help of our neighbor; his special friend, he not only put venison in the freezer; he learned taxidermy and put his Buck up on the living room wall.

Patrick was proud and so was I!

Patty was very accepted in this rural area. All of the other kids greatly enjoyed Patrick. I began to notice, shortly after moving to this area; no matter how friendly I was to the people in the Village—with a few exceptions, they were not friendly to me in return.

I wondered about this, however; we did not live in the Village and we did have some true, wonderful friend's right down our road.

This became apparent to me when I attended my son's basketball games in the Village. No one said "Hello" to me; I found myself sitting all alone watching my son and his team play basketball. This also happened to me at the school awards ceremonies. I continued to be friendly saying "Hello" to people, holding doors open for them; only a few returned the friendliness and kindness. I began to hear the word, "outsider" from some of the people in my own area along the inland lake.

"Outsider"; this was a term the people in the Village used.

"Outsider" meaning; you are not one of us—you are new blood and we do not welcome you here.

I asked members of my family to attend the home games for basketball with me; they attended many times. Family members also attended the awards ceremonies; I did not feel so all alone. My son sat with us at the awards ceremonies; he could not be with me during the games—he was playing!

Aurora Borealis

I tried for many years to be friendly with the Village People. One day I awoke and took on a different attitude. I would 'only' go into the Village when I really had to; I 'no' longer bothered to say Hello or do the things I had in the past.

Patrick was accepted; I attributed this to the fact that kids are more open minded and accepting than adults. I felt rejected; my son felt accepted!

I was not a bar person; I was a homebody and my goal in life was to raise Patrick to be a success. Patrick would tell me; if you would go to the bars you would meet someone and people. I was not a drinker and this was not the lifestyle for me. Besides; who would I really meet in this Village in a bar?

I have mentioned living on a small set income; another reason I stayed home was this shortage of money. I did not want my son Patrick to go without; I would give him all the money I had. He had to keep going in school; in all his sporting programs and other interests.

My injuries, winter, and lack of money prohibited me from attending my son's away basketball games. Patty was the basketball player—he needed the money; it was given to him.

CHAPTER 4

JUNIOR HIGH SCHOOL

BASKETBALL

Junior High School Basketball was incredibly time consuming and costly.

There were summer basketball camps; if you did not attend; you could not be on the team for the upcoming school year.

Girls Basketball started at the beginning of the school year; Boy's Basketball began towards the hardest time of the year for me; the beginning of winter.

Along with my neck injuries from my auto accident; winter brought with it the onset of incredibly painful arthritis.

We would wake up extra early in the morning; I would get breakfast ready as Patty would shower and get ready for his school day.

Down the road we would go; early in the morning to get Patrick to school. The school bus did not leave this early, it was up to me; to get him there on time.

Before the start of the school day—Patty and the basketball team would go through conditioning practice.

Next; his school day would begin; after the school day was over; there was the actual basketball practice. Patty would call me and down the road I would go to get him at the school.

Home we would go; I would make dinner as he did all his homework.

We did this daily ritual over and over again during his Junior High days.

The washer and dryer were working overtime as my son's home and away uniforms had to be cleaned constantly—along with his athletic socks.

Basketball shoes were incredibly expensive.

I did not mind doing any of these things— what did bother me were the away games.

Patrick would arrive home most of the time in the early morning hours; I would wait up until he called and down the road I would go through ice storms, snow storms whatever 'Mother Nature' handed out to get My Son.

Later on his coaches would give him a ride home; this made it easier on me in one way, however; harder in another.

I began to worry about My Son not getting enough rest, sleep and food.

On the weekends he stayed home; he had a chance to get the necessary rest; sleep and nutrition needed to keep up his grueling schedule.

It appeared to me as if My Son was being 'worn way to thin' by the school he attended.

Patty did really well at the game of basketball during his Junior High Years.

Just, as I thought he and our budget would have time to recover; the coaches pressured him to run track. I wanted Patty to pursue his studies, rest, and have time to eat meals on a regular schedule.

The school and the coaches wanted him to continue on with this grueling schedule; I considered this asking far too much of me and my son.

Despite it all, Patrick was always on the Honor Roll, did well at both basketball and track; managed to catch up on his rest and diet requirements during the summer breaks from this rural Village School.

Before we knew it; Patrick was in his High School years.

The coaches from the school pressured both me and my son—he tried Football; we both realized this was not his game. I thanked "The Good Lord" when he decided one football season was enough. Patrick was not the 'right build' for the game of Football.

Basketball was Patty's game! He excelled in his High School Years at Basketball—played Varsity Basketball for three years. To say I was a proud Mother watching My Son play the position of Starting Point Guard would be stating it too mildly. Some games; Patrick would score more points himself; than the points of the entire other team.

We went through the same grueling schedule for quite some time.

The before school conditioning; the school day; the after school practice; the expenses for the laundering of the uniforms the athletic socks and shoes—the money it took for all the away games. Once again I did not mind sacrificing of myself to see My Son Patrick becoming such a success in his life. This is what a Mother is all about! What bothered me was my son's lack of rest, sleep, and time to eat a good healthy meal. My greatest concern was his arriving home in the early morning hours; only getting a few hours sleep; then starting another grueling day all over again. In my mind; this school was teaching My Son to 'burn the candle at both ends.'

On the weekend; I would actually take the telephone off the hook; I did this so no one would bother My Son. I wanted to cook for him and fuel his young developing body with the nutritious meals he needed. I wanted Patrick to slow his body down over the weekend, get some rest and be able to relax and mend his young body.

Throughout all the High School Basketball, Track and later High School Golf—I began to sense that this Village—the school, and the people in the area were taking my son away from me. I began to feel lonely; I knew My Son Patrick was developing into a young man; at the same time I felt like I was slowly losing him to them.

I recall one day going into the Village to get my hair cut. I needed it cut desperately; it was easier with my medical problems to drive into the Village in the winter; than to drive a greater distance on the icy, snowy dangerous winter roads.

As the young beautician was cutting my hair; she said to me; "You know, you can't hang on to him forever." "Isn't it time you start letting him go?" On my short drive home and for days afterward I wondered what she meant by this. Of course, I knew I could not hang on to My Son, Patrick forever. Patty, at this time was only 15 years of age! The more I thought about her comments, the more it troubled me!

On another occasion, I was taking some large bags of garbage into the Service Station with the dumpster. Patty was along with me.

My Son knew how much pain I endured from my neck injuries; he would do all the heavy lifting and carrying—when he was around.

Patrick was between the ages of 15 and 16 at the time.

The store clerk said to me: "Wow, what are you going to do—when your Son is No Longer Around." Another statement that bothered my mind! Why did these people in this rural Village keeping making statements to me like this about my son, Patrick; he was still young?

CHAPTER 5

'OUR STRONG MOTHER SON

LOVE BOND'

Despite the hectic high School schedule; Patrick and I shared a strong Mother-Son Love bond. At this time there was an advertising campaign about 'have you hugged your child today and told your child you loved them?'

I turned this around and Patrick and I had fun with it.

Each time he left the house – I would holler "Stop, Wait, haven't you forgotten something" Patty would stop he knew why.

I would say; 'hey have you hugged your mom today.'

At the door we would give each other a tight hug and I would give him a little kiss on the cheek; later as he grew taller than me; on

45

the neck. I would always say; "I Love you Patty" and in return I would hear; "I Love You Too Ma." This special little ritual was always carried on.

We had many happy times together during the high school years. We had three pets, a Little Parakeet, a little dog and a medium sized dog. My son Patrick shared my love for pets, our home in the Northwoods and all the beauty and wildlife that surrounded us.

The Holidays were always happy fun filled times for the two of us. At times we went into my hometown on the holidays and spent them with family. Other times we chose to just stay home, kick back and have quiet peaceful times together.

We had a mutual friend; a young man, a couple years older than Patrick.

He would come down to our place; we spent many happy hours watching movies and playing card games together.

Patty was still too young to drive; I would let our friend take my car into the Village to rent the movies and get the munchies and soda. The three of us loved these fun filled special times we shared together.

There were sleepovers; I would awake to lumps all over the floors. Some of the lumps were covered with dog blankets! Some of the lumps had dogs on top of them!

The house would be filled with noise and excitement. Young boys everywhere; being boys; silly, smiling and laughing! How these days warmed My Heart.

Two winters in a row—I had two different surgeries.

I planned everything in advance including having a freezer and refrigerator filled with food and pre-cooked meals. I could not make it up the stairs for awhile so I slept in the living room on the hide-a-bed.

Before school each morning; My Son would make certain I had everything I needed close to me; including the phone. On his lunch time at school; He would call to make certain I was alright. Patrick bestowed the same Love on me that I showered upon him.

With my son's caring and loving help; I healed rapidly from both surgeries.

Shortly after my first surgery that took place in the winter, I grew restless and could not stay in bed any longer; despite my doctor's orders.

I bundled up for winter and went outside. Taking a shovel, I cleared the snow away from in front of the garage door, the doors to the house and the mailbox.

Coming back into the house; I changed into my bed clothing and got right back onto the hide-a-bed under the warm covers.

My son returned from school and came directly into the living room.

Looking at me he said;' "Would you mind telling me how the snow got moved while I was in school." Patrick was very upset when he listened to me tell him; it was me; I was restless.

My second surgery was for a Hernia Repair. Both Patrick and I knew how this hernia came into being!

In the State of Michigan there is a leveled driver's license system. First the young driver must complete a driver's training course; next they must have a certain number of hours behind the wheel with an adult in the car. Next; comes the actual driver's test—this for me and Patrick was a great concern. We only had one car and at this time the blinkers would not work right. Patrick and I jerry-rigged the blinker system; I sat in the back seat with the instructor up front in the passenger seat; with

Patrick behind the wheel. This was an extensive driving test. I sat quietly in the back seat; you were not allowed to speak. I did not want to speak; I prayed; yes; the blinkers did not let us down. Patrick passed his test. Right after the test on the drive home; they did begin to give us a hard time.

The next step in Michigan is for the young driver; to drive during certain hours; finally they obtain a full license as Patrick acquired.

CHAPTER 6

PATRICK'S 17th BIRTHDAY AND

JUNIOR YEAR OF HIGH SCHOOL

Aurora Borealis

Shortly after Patrick's 17th Birthday and his Junior Year of High School; the pace of his life and mine became greatly accelerated.

Ending Track and the regional finals; Science trips to a College City for the Engineering and Science Fair.

Patrick loved these gatherings of High School students from all over Northern Michigan.

Only certain students from each school were chosen. The ones that were chosen; had even more to do!

This was time consuming; as 'The Group' was assigned Engineering and Science projects; highly time consuming projects. At times; they created bridges; elaborate bridges. The bridges could only weigh a minute amount and the weights they held were high.

These bridges were created out of 'toothpicks.'

Away they went to the College City and the fair.

Many, many, beautiful medals arrived home accompanying a smiling, happy, proud face! Patrick and his 'team' had scored well!

Close to the ending of each High School year; there were awards ceremonies.

One for academic achievement; one for athletic abilities.

Yes; we attended both together each and every year.

Patrick did well at both categories.

A member of The National Honor Society; in his Junior Year; Patty did well.

Many, many certificates and trophies also came into Our Home!

What Patrick and I had reached out to achieve was 'coming true.'

We were both so proud; not arrogantly; just proud!

Patrick was succeeding at everything he reached out and touched.

My Heart felt happiness; we did not have much money; we were "Making It Happen."

During My Son's Junior year; I took on a mortgage on our home; I knew the last years of High school were costly. I wanted Patrick to not go without.

He worked so long and hard; he deserved what I gave him.

The sports banquet in his Junior year; created a very difficult situation.

Patrick and His Father kept in contact; through the form of letters.

With my prodding; Patty would write His Father a letter and inform him of the up coming events, including Basketball games and track runs.

My ex-husband was going to attend. Patty was happy; there was a problem; My Son and I had to discuss.

My ex-husband could not 'see' me.

I knew in My Heart; how I too had struggled; such as Patrick; to achieve his successes.

I was going to be at the Village school.

Working out in the yard; I watched the time.

Hearing a vehicle pull into our driveway; I walked around the side of the house.

My Sister and her Husband had arrived.

I rode to the school with them for the Sports Banquet.

Patrick was to meet his Father after school; spend some time with him; and the two of them would attend the banquet.

Getting out of the van; I looked down the street and saw My Beautiful Son riding up with His Father.

The three of us started walking towards the school.

As I walked; I looked.

I saw my ex-husband reach over and Give Patty a 'hug' and a 'kiss.'

Next; the car drove past us and away.

Patrick came walking towards us; with an odd look on his face.

His Aunt asked; "Patrick, where is Your Father going."

Patty answered; with a combination of sadness, happiness and tears.

"He saw My Mother; gave me a hug and a kiss."

"He told me he was going to cry;" "he could not stay."

Patty also said; "He's already crying!"

"There is good news," said Patty.

"Look; what Pa gave me for my 17th Birthday!"

Patrick was given a cashier's check for $5000 for his own vehicle.

This was good news and bad, worrisome news for me as a 'single parent.'

Patrick and I chose a car for him; A Ford Taurus.

The car and insurance had to be placed in my name; My Son was still too young.

When Patrick turned 18; the car would legally belong to him.

His Father gave him the money for a vehicle; telling Patrick; "it's up to Your Mother to insure it."

This car and the Michigan leveled licensing system caused me many worries and stress. Patrick was on 'top of the world.'

His Mother was worried.

In my mind; he was too young to have his own vehicle.

High School Graduation would have been a

much better time for such an expensive 'gift.'

CHAPTER 7

PATRICK'S ONE PROM

Patrick attended one prom during his high school years.

Proms take some time and money to organize.

I was out in the yard; weeding the flower garden, when the Limo and all of the many young people arrived.

A rented Limo and driver; these kids went first class to the prom!

I cleaned my hands, got my camera, and took photos of each and every couple, also group shots. Not to forget the limo and the cute, young woman driver.

Patrick's bow-tie gave him a humorous hard time.

Young woman tried—the bow-tie would not co-operate.

I tried—no way!

The limo driver tried repeatedly.

Away they went to the events proceeding the prom—the prom and the gathering afterward.

Away went Patrick; bow-tie slightly dangling and way off center.

All; smiling and waving at me in great happiness.

My son had made arrangements with me. It was agreed he could spend the night on the Island—he would leave his car at the land side of the ferry dock.

We agreed upon his time; when he was due home in the morning.

I awoke the next morning, took care of myself and the pets. Next I went outside to do some gardening.

Patty's arrival time came and went; and went; and went.

I called a neighbor; a great friend and together we went to the Ferry Dock.

Having keys; I started the car and drove it home.

My son arrived home in the early afternoon; there was an exchange of words between the two of us. Yes; he had not been driving. Yes; he had not followed the rules and had broken his promise to me.

Many words were exchanged back and forth between the two of us; as there was a strong smell of alcohol radiating from My Son.

This greatly saddened me and hurt my 'heart.' Patrick and I had many conversations about Prom night. Mother was not going to tolerate this underage drinking and Patrick understood.

His Mother was against underage drinking and those of age who furnish it to them!

CHAPTER 8

PATRICK BEGAN WORKING AT

THE AGE OF 16

My Son, Patrick began working at the age of 16. This was an incredibly hard summer for us; financially.

There was a lengthy strike downstate where my ex worked.

We lived on my alimony and Patty's child support.

My ex decided he was not working; would not walk the strike line; and did not want to pay us our weekly support.

I was forced to turn to the state, they helped us after awhile. Later; I repaid them more than they gave me and my son in assistance at that time.

Aurora Borealis

This is the summer when Patrick began spending a lot of time on the Island.

Patrick found himself a summer job on the Island washing dishes; his best friend was one of the cooks.

I would drive Patty to the ferry dock with his bicycle; he would get on the ferry and ride his bike for a good 15 miles to his work.

I worried every night; I knew he had a light on his bike; light or not; those back roads were dark and dangerous!

He would ride his bike after work the fifteen miles to the ferry; take the ferry over to the mainland and then pedal the extra distance home.

The owner 'got wind' of this and all quickly changed.

I would drive Patrick to the ferry; another employee would get him there and drive him to work. After work he was given a ride to the ferry and I would be there on the 'other side' waiting for My Son.

Patrick contributed greatly to the household that extremely difficult summer.

To say I was proud of my young son would be stating it too mildly.

We survived the hardships that summer—it built even more 'character' for the two of us.

Our money eventually resumed on a regular schedule.

In his Junior and Senior Years; Patrick acquired a wonderful work position.

He worked on a golf course as an attendant.

'His good friend;' who taught him many things; turned him on to 'the game of golf.'

This gave My Son the opportunity to practice the game of golf over and over and over again. He would still play basketball his Senior Year; golf, however; was the game he really loved. Patrick told me over and over again. "Ma, if you think I am good at basketball, I am a natural at the game of golf; it comes so easy to me."

The following year at the age of 17; I took my son on a summer get-a-way vacation. We had the greatest time; yes; I watched My Son Golf. He was going to golf 18 holes by himself; with me and the camera riding along; watching; and taking photos.

He did not golf alone; a much older man came along.

The two of them golfed together; both me; and the other fellow could not believe 'our eyes.'

Patrick won the 18 holes. Easily!

What a wonderful mini vacation Mother and Son shared.

Patrick earned good money at his new work, his wages and the tremendous tips. He continued to contribute a large portion of his money to the household.

A Good Son!

Patrick began spending more and more time on the Island.

Spending nights on the Island; cut down his work expenses, the cost of the ferry was expensive; his workplace did not pay the fare.

More and more, I began to feel as if my son was gone 'from me' more than he should have been.

CHAPTER 9

SENIOR YEAR OF HIGH SCHOOL

My son's Senior Year of High school; flew by!

So many, many details in the Senior Year.

Patrick was voted Homecoming King by the Senior Class.

I attended the football game; it was announced Patrick was indeed Homecoming King along with his Queen. I took photos of this once in a lifetime event.

I was proud, however; I did not mention it; only to family and close friends.

Becoming Homecoming King took place on Friday Night.

I went home after the game and My Son came home later that night.

Going about our lives as normal, the following Monday I did some banking business in the Village.

When I arrived at the bank; I greeted the tellers with my normal friendliness; I was happy.

Another woman; I knew, and liked entered the bank.

All of a sudden; I could not believe what was being said to me.

The woman; who entered the bank; turned and congratulated me on Patrick being Homecoming King. I thanked her and turned to take care of business.

The teller's face turned red with anger.

Looking straight at me she said;' He did not deserve to be Homecoming King." "I thought he looked little a little kid up there on the float—just like a damned little kid."

Abruptly; she left the room.

Me; and the other two women looked at each other; not one of us picked up on the tellers' behavior or comments.

The teller had a son who graduated this year along with Patrick.

The parents of the Senior's did not decide who would take the positions of King and Queen. This decision was made by the other students.

The parents would have made certain one of 'their own' was chosen.

Later at home; I called my neighbor; my good friend, to speak with her about this occurrence.

Her reply came fast and easy.

"He's an 'outsider' Patrick is not one of them."

Senior Basketball went well, Patty's best year for the game was; no doubt; his Junior Year.

The game was completely understood by Patrick. He had it down!

Patrick and the team did well this year; it all came to proof in the athletic awards ceremony in the Spring.

Graduation was drawing near and there were many things needing mine and my son's attention.

Patrick graduated' top boy' in his class, member of the National Honor Society Gold Cord. Many certificates, scholarships and plaques.

The plaques were his; others were located in the school; each year another named is added. This would be Patrick; for his excellence in both athletic and academic achievement.

Graduation time arrived; his Father showed up; spent time with Patrick and then left. He did not attend the actual ceremony. Patrick had me, family members and many friends of mine and My Son's.

I spent lots of time and money and praying for the right weather for his party.

The graduation party was held in the backyard. The "Good Lord' answered my prayers—the weather was beautiful. Bright, Blue, Sunny Skies.

Most of the people invited; arrived; spent time with me and Patty and left.

Patrick had his girl there with him.

I noticed right away; My Son had a worried look on his face.

I kept asking him; 'Is there something wrong Patrick?'

His answer was "No." "I'm just tired!"

84

Finally; four young men arrived. Great I thought; now the young people are coming! Perhaps this is what Patrick is worried over?

The four young men came; did not stay long and left.

No other teenagers came to Patrick's Graduation Party.

The four young men entered the garage; I saw my Son In Law follow them in. My son in law said" Hey there boys;" "Aren't you all in the wrong tub?" "The one with the sodas; boys; the sodas."

They picked at their food; had a couple of drinks of soda looked at Patrick and began to leave.

My Son looked at them; next at me.

Patrick said in a sad way; "See, didn't I tell you the way she is?"

My son's graduation party was a big flop in my eyes. It took place shortly after the graduation itself; early in the day; and yes; I would not allow underage drinking on my premises; they would have to drive away.

NO! NO! NO!

Patrick was not too pleased with me, for quite sometime afterwards. "Thanks for ruining my Graduation Party Mom." "Thanks"

I later learned; the fun, underage drinking parties for Graduation took place in the late evening. Patrick and his girl left his party; they went to other parties; He was home quite early the next morning.

Things were not quite ever the same between the two of us.

After graduation Patrick worked at the Golf Course. He did his normal routine; wanting to stay over there more and more. To save the daily cost of the ferry; I was told! I began to see less and less of My Son.

College time arrived and off he went. Patty, failed to tell me he was not ready to attend College. I began to notice him; coming and going from home more and more. One day; we sat down in the kitchen and talked.

He finally told me "The Truth." He was tired of studying; he pointed out the window and said "I want to be out there." "Out there in the world; working,"

We agreed to this; I was not going to pressure My Son into something he did not want to do; was not ready for at this time.

Work at certain times in Northern Michigan is hard to find.

Most of the work; is tourist related and begins when the Spring Thaw is over.

Patrick worked on a ferry; part time; and also helped right in our living area. He was a helper; building pole barns. He helped with the construction of three. He would tell me; "I Love it; I'm learning so much." "I love working with wood!" Elderly neighbor women; would call with a problem around their place; out of the house; Patrick would go;

to help them. Patty loved people; there was no question in my mind about this.

Next, He secured full time employment on the Island. This job was working with wood. The Spring Thaw was over; between working one full time job and working a part time job on a ferry; he did not forget—his Love of Golf.

Patrick fit in golfing on two men's leagues and this he also Loved.

"Wait and see;" Patty would tell me. "Wait and see Ma." "I am going to be on the' PGA Tour' one day Ma." I am not saying I will be on the top; not for a long time; even if I come in last Ma; I will still make lots of money."

"I am that good of a golfer Ma."

Many, many people mentioned Patrick's golfing abilities to me.

They all compared Patrick to Professional Golfers and said "There is the next Tiger Woods."

Where we resided up North; they would advertise in Alabama; 'The Robert Trent Jones Golf Trails.' Patrick and I would watch these commercials together; over the winter. I would always tell him: "Next year Patty; I am going to take you there."

"Let's see how good a golfer you are Son?"

Patrick would always smile back at me; as he practiced his golfing in the house over the winter. White golf balls were always being 'chipped' around the floors in our home.

My Son knew I was a Mother of 'Her Word.'

He knew he would be golfing there the following summer.

CHAPTER 10

EARLY WINTER OF THE YEAR

2000

During the early winter of the year 2000; My Son and I went on three different short trips.

The first occasion was when Patty came home and found me shaking and in tears.

He held me and asked "What's wrong Ma.?"

Through my tears I answered, "OH Patty— I just got some bad news on my favorite Aunt." "She is all alone in the hospital where you attended College briefly." "All alone and having pacemaker surgery." "She is scared and has pneumonia too."

Patrick said to me, "Get ready and I will go fuel up the car; I will drive you Ma."

Twice My Son drove me further into the winter wonderland to see 'our special aunt. She mended well; this took some time. My Son; I learned, was an excellent driver. He loved both me and his special aunt very much.

Christmas was approaching and Patty and I normally spent it at home.

We loved Christmas this way—it was our tradition.

As Christmas approached he said to me; "Ma, let's go downstate this year and see our Family." "I will drive Ma; no problem."

Aurora Borealis

On Christmas Eve day away we went; with a car full of presents and food.

Everyone was happy to see us, my daughter, Son in law; granddaughter and ex brother in law too. Oh yes; Patrick was an uncle too.

Together we had a fun filled, wonderful, memorable Christmas in the year 2000.

Patrick took my car and drove to see his Father on Christmas Eve; also on Christmas Day. On Christmas Eve they talked and watched a movie together.

On Christmas Day, Patty went to see His Father again. He brought His Father two covered plates filled with Christmas dinner.

On the drive back to 'The Northern Part of Michigan'; we listened to music. My Son and I shared a Love for music and at times we would 'rock' our house when a song came on the radio that we both loved. One of these songs was called "Shooting Star"; there were many others! We talked on our drive back; we both felt so happy about the time we spent together with our loved ones downstate.

CHAPTER 11

'THE STATE OF ALABAMA

In late January into early February of 2001;

I went on a planned two week vacation to the

State of Alabama.

This was agreed upon between My Son and I.

I was seriously considering relocating to

Alabama; for health reasons.

Of Utmost Importance; I wanted My Up In

Coming PGA Tour "Son' to practice his love

of 'golf' throughout the entire year.

Hard to achieve; in the high, snow banks of

life in Northern Michigan.

I had a feeling Patty would Love Alabama;

secure employment in' no time at all'.

99

Patrick was extremely intelligent; he already knew so much.

He would be in a much better region for golfing.

This was My Son's real, true Love in his Life.

Golf!

Shortly after returning home; we had some real cleaning to do. Yes; there were parties at the house while I was gone.

'Underage, drinking parties.' Booze!

'The down fall of many, young people.'

The cleaning was accomplished; throughout it all; there were the unpleasant; 'this is putting it mildly again,' conversations and arguments over 'underage drinking' and driving. I was Not Happy after I returned from Alabama!

One morning; a Private Investigator came to the door. I was going in and out; loading the car for a drive; to do some laundry and get a few things.

I called into the living room from the kitchen, "Oh Patrick," there is a Private Investigator here to talk with you."

Now, what was this about?

My son walked smiling into the kitchen; shook the investigator's hand and introduced himself.

My comment was; "Well, I don't know what this is all about." Patrick," "I am out of here, you two enjoy your conversation, 'have fun'" "Patrick; I will talk to you when I get back.!"

I went and did the laundry; picked up what we needed. Returning home Patty came out and unloaded the car; carrying the things into our home.

We spoke right away about the investigator.

Patrick, said to me; It's no big deal, there was some violence at a New Year's Eve party in a distant, neighboring community and some destruction of property."

"Don't worry about it Ma." "I will handle it!"

My Son was Nineteen; I had to give him the necessary room to grow into a man; and the chance to 'spread his wings'. Patrick was a little too 'easy going' for my liking. I had learned much earlier in my days here; I would be 'trampled' over in this area. I became an 'aggressive, assertive, independent female.'

I remember being in Patty's room, putting laundry away, gathering up other items.

It was then; I saw the cell phone.

A cell phone; hum; he must have got this while I was in Alabama.

I wondered if Patrick could afford to have a cell phone?

My Son and I spoke about the cell phone.

He took on a defensive attitude—not like my Patty.

He said to me," The only thing I can tell you is;" "I need to have this phone!"

"I need it." "Don't ask me anything more" "I can't tell you!"

As I stood there looking at My Son; I looked deep into His Eyes.

Something was really wrong and as His Mother I 'sensed" it.

What was happening to My Son?

Later I was to learn, after reading some court exams; yes it was another' under age drinking party' on New Years Eve 2000.

There was destruction of property; My Son and his friends from out 'our way' could have been seriously injured or worse 'that early morning.'

All these teenagers had been doing some heavy drinking!

Violence erupted over the competition of High School Basketball.

High School Basketball; in out of the way rural communities. I was completely unaware; 'Basketball' could become so competitive to the degree of violence.

My son and his friends from out their way; were in a car, frantically attempting to get' the hell' out of there.

They were blocked in; in the driveway.

The car and the teenagers in it; 'it was reported' was being rocked, kicked and shook; to the point of being like 'out of' a Michigan State University Riot!

While reading these reports; I learned the Private Investigator came to see My Son; for a reason. He was told by many in the area; "You want to talk to an honest young man;" go see Patrick.

The teenagers from Patty's area; all decided upon one story on the way home; they would stick with this invented version.

Patrick made a few trips into the larger distance town. He would not tell me where he was going. Something serious I sensed from his face. I found out; My Son; was going to the Prosecuting Attorney's Office to talk with them!

Patrick's smiling, happy face; at times held a troubled, worried look.

Much, much, later; I learned there was going to be a jury trial.

My Son; was to be 'subpeoned ' in towards the end; along with one other young woman from his area.

They were the two; who were deemed to be so well known and well liked by many; the two who would 'tell the truth.' This would never take place; as 'one' of the two honest young teenagers would not be able to appear!

Shortly after arriving back from Alabama; the Investigator, the cell phone and my terrifying re-occurring nightmares told me something was really wrong—something to do with MY SON!

CHAPTER 12

MY FRIGHTENING NIGHTMARES

My son Patrick and I shared a very strong Mother-Son 'Love Bond.'

There were young women in his life; three, I know of for certain.

One of these young women; the one who he, ' held deep in his heart' would soon come to be with me and hold my hand.

My son was an easy going, young man. He was pretty much the same as all the other young people. However; he did excel at everything he 'touched.'

Patty was soft hearted; would feel bad if a bird hit his car or later his truck.

He would always tell me "Ma; I do not kill things." Even a wild bird dying would upset him; he felt guilt!

After the Private Investigator came to visit Patrick; I began to experience the most frightening nightmares.

These nightmares were horrible and re-occurring.

Always; the same nightmare.

I would wake up; always around 3:00 A.M. shaking and trembling out of control; wet with heavy tears and sweating profusely.

A couple of times; My Son came upstairs and woke me.

"Ma, Ma, wake up; you are having a terrible nightmare."

Holding me and calming me, Patrick would give me a little kiss on the cheek and tell me "it's alright Ma."

I would look at him and say, "OH Patrick; you are alright!"

Patty would tell me "of course I am alright Ma", please get some sleep.

I told my son the nightmares were about him; I never told him any more.

I should have!

113

The nightmares were always the same; a law enforcement official would come to the door and tell me that My Beautiful Son; Patrick had lost his life in an auto accident.

Due to my age and menopause; I thought these terrible nightmares; I kept having were associated with menopause and night sweats.

During the days that followed; I would continue to remember the nightmares as I looked at My Son; I kept sensing something was heavy on his mind.

Towards the end of July 2001, Patrick came home from golfing on one of his men's golf leagues—happy as a lark!

He was to have his name in this week's newspaper for his golfing success that afternoon at golf. Once again; He was proud and His Mother was too.

We anxiously awaited that edition of the newspaper to arrive.

Patrick also mentioned to me; something about a distant, neighboring community man.

Patty said he and his partner; reported this fellow had shot a hole in one.

"Ma" he said, "None of the rest of us believe it." "No one else but the two of them saw it."

Patrick and I also discussed something else on that early evening the end of July 2001.

Patrick wanted to stop working on the ferry.

My Son, told me of all, the' not so nice' remarks he got from the very start of this work position.

The remarks and comments came from older men.

"Hey kid, how did you get this job?"

My Son would answer in his normal good natured manner, "I applied for it."

Patrick, told me these comments were coming at him more frequently.

My Son appeared worried and troubled; it was decided he would let this job go!

CHAPTER 13

MY SON WAS WORRIED AND

TROUBLED

My son was worried and troubled; something 'heavy' was on his mind.

We went about life as usual, On Thursday night before going to bed; I packed his lunch into his cooler along with many bottles of water, juice pacs and soda.

Patrick upon waking in the morning; knew where to get his lunchbox cooler and drinks before leaving for work.

I did not get up with him on that Friday morning.

When I awoke, it was a hot, humid day in the Northwoods of Michigan.

119

I went into another, distant community that morning to run some errands; to do some shopping for food and supplies.

I thought of My Son many times throughout the day.

Shopping; I bought him many of the foods he loved; also personal care items he needed.

I cooked out of the grill that early evening; I knew Patty had stopped to practice golf after work and would not be home for awhile.

The neighbor called; knowing that my allergies were better 'on the water' he asked me to go fishing with him. I agreed!

I had caught a 'pretty nice' walleye earlier in the season: I wanted to get an even bigger and more impressive one.

I finished cooking dinner; carefully wrapped My son's on a plate; and placed it in the refrigerator.

I took care of the pets; from the high heat and humidity.

Next, I left My Son a note (our normal procedure) towards each other.

We would always leave this notes taped on the kitchen table.

In the note I told Patrick; Out on the Lake Fishing—hope I get the 'big one." "I love You", Mom!

121

When I arrived home a smile lit up my face as I read the note My Son has left me in return. "Ma, dinner was great." I'm going into another 'distant' community for the "Friday Night Street dance."

"See you later tonight or tomorrow."

"Love You Mom, Patrick."

Knowing that My Son and most all of the young people were doing some drinking—My Son promised me; he would 'stay where he was.'

This was our deal!

I had tried over and over again to discourage this' underage drinking.'

Knowing; it was taking place, we had to discuss it; and this was the deal we had struck! "Stay where you are; promise me Patrick." My Son promised me and I believed him!

I went to bed that night happy—I did not catch the great fish; still I was happy.

Around 3:A.M. it happened to me again!

I awoke; wide awake; trembling and shaking out of control.

All sweaty; with heavy, heavy wet tears; tears that happened to me 'in my sleep.'

Aurora Borealis

My HEART was in my throat, I went downstairs and looked in My Son's bedroom. OH God; he was not there!

I thought 'calm down' another one; of those horrible nightmares.

I splashed water on my face and used some allergy eye drops.

I went outside in the yard; looking up, I again noticed the beautiful large orange-shaded 'full moon.' The neighbor and I while out on the lake; kept watching this incredibly beautiful moon.

There were stars and constellations visible to the 'eye' everywhere that night.

The skies were magnificent in the early, Saturday morning hours.

Still; I sensed 'something' was terribly wrong!

I went back into the house; back to my bed.

I believed My Son had spent the night in this distant community after the Community Days Friday Night Street Dance.

Somehow; I managed to fall asleep once again.

My Heart awoke me with a jerky start.

There was the sound of sirens going down 'our road.'

Running to the upstairs window; I looked out.

My Son's truck was not in the yard.

Oh God!

I almost fell running down the stairs; he was not in his room.

I went into the kitchen looked up at "Jesus." I Looked at him long and hard!

Next, I freshened my face; took care of Patrick's pets.

I kept shaking and trembling; wishing my body would stop!

My ears heard a vehicle pulling into the driveway.

Again; I looked up at "Jesus."

I heard a police radio in our driveway.

Oh My God! My Heart!

I raced to the door; shaking out of control; Oh God!

An officer of the law walked past the door—looked into our beautiful back yard; then came back to the door.

I spoke; as well as I could; "Officer are you here about My Son?"

127

He said "Yes Ma'am" "I am; would you open the door and we will sit at the table and talk."

Before he even came through the door; I said; "Officer is MY SON DEAD?"

He did not answer me.

We sat only a brief second: He told me MY Son had been in an auto accident sometime around 3:00 in the early morning. Three in the morning; as in all 'My Nightmares!'

I jumped up with tears rolling down; My voice cracked and my throat was dry; as I said"Officer; "IS MY SON DEAD?"

He replied with tears; "Yes Ma'am—HE IS!"

CHAPTER 14

I COULD NOT BREATHE

I could not breathe. I began hyperventilating.

My eyes went to the kitchen wall; there I looked at My Son's graduation photo.

His graduation was in May of 2000; this was the beginning of August 2001!

Oh God; I was in the hallway; leaning over a wicker basket.

Doubled over; could not catch my breath.

Oh God; My Son never made it home!

My NIGHTMARES 'Came True.'

I remembered walking back into the kitchen; the officer asked me, "Do you have a bad heart, Ma'am?"

"No" I answered weakly. 'I just can't breathe."

"Ma'am do you have a medical condition" Do you take medication for something?"

"Yes," I said.

"Ma'am; please take your medication now."

I did!

Ma'am is there someone you want me to call for you?"

"No."

"I will call My Sister."

I barely remember the conversation.

I do recall; calling My Daughter, Patrick's Sister.

131

My Son In Law answered the phone.

He told Patrick's Sister.

I could hear My Daughter screaming and crying out of control in the background.

They all were!

The officer was in a 'hurry.' "Can I take you someplace close" "Is there someone in the area I can take you to?"

"Yes, my neighbors."

I hardly remember the short drive; I got out frantic; I still could not breathe or see for my tears.

I saw my neighbor walking up; I ran towards him screaming his name.

He came close and threw his arms around me and I shouted; "My Son is dead!"

Tears rolled down his cheeks and I fell on the ground; I could not stand.

All of a sudden; I realized I had to see MY SON!

I wanted to drive myself to the accident scene.

The officer begged my neighbor to not let me go to the accident scene.

I said; "He is My Son;" "I have to be there with him."

I heard the officer tell my neighbor; there is too much going on at the scene. A gruesome sight with many emergency vehicles there; including the 'jaws of life.'

I stayed at my neighbors shaking, trembling and crying so hard; the tears burnt my cheeks. My Sister arrived and took over. She has been trained in her life to be 'in control.'

There was 'NO" in control for me; not now!

CHAPTER 15

TEENAGERS; THE ACCIDENT SCENE; ALL 'THE OTHERS'

Some of what happened right after that is a 'blur' to me.

I remember my sister and her son arriving; before them; My, great friend and neighbor came down; jumped out of her truck; ran in, and grabbed me tight.

We cried together.

She was as 'in shock' as me.

I remember a car of teenage girls drove up. I went outside; I did not know who they were.

Turned out; they were part of the crowd from the area; the crowd My Son Patty was with for 'The Distant Community Days Friday Night Street Dance.'

136

Only one of these girls spoke; and looked at me.

I could not catch the other's eyes; they kept staring at the ground and would not speak.

The spokesman for the group; told me some things on that late Saturday morning the beginning of August 2001.

She stated that none of them understood "what happened to Pat?"

"Pat, was an excellent driver;" she said; "He could handle his beer well."

She told me; she saw My Son in the early morning hours on that exact highway.

She had come back from the Distant Community one way; stated my son had come back along another route.

She told me; her and Pat had both pulled over and spoken; not too far away from the accident scene.

"How was My Son?" I said.

She answered, "Pat was fine; the other kid with him was 'passed out.'

I remembered then; the officer told me—both My Son and his friend; both died in the accident.

I spoke with the young woman as well as I could do at this time.

I was crying so hard; speech was difficult.

Right after they left; a vehicle with young men arrived at our house.

They too, had been with My Son and the crowd from out 'our way' that night.

This part I remember 'only too well.'

I was crying hard—the pain was overwhelming for me.

I remember one of them was the speaker.

None of them would look at me.

All of them stared at the ground!

They all stared at the ground.

While they stared at the ground; they all did a 'strange' thing with their feet in the ground! A really strange thing!

A sad, crying, young women came to me next.

I recalled her; she was once my son's girlfriend.

We hugged, cried and spoke briefly.

She later tried to help me; with 'NO' success.

Next to arrive; was the young woman that Patrick really loved.

A beautiful young woman; she had seen Patrick for about a half hour; on that Friday night and Saturday morning.

She had hugged him and they spoke.

This was not the young woman; My Son spent Friday night into Saturday morning with!

This young woman; (The Love In My Son's Heart); stayed with me and the family from that moment on all the way through. My Son's Love and His Mother held hands through all the upcoming incredibly, painful events.

I did not ask; I TOLD My Sister ; "You have to take me there."

141

"Right now!"

My nephew drove and My Son's love was with us.

The area was police cordoned off. I could hardly get my legs to move. All they did was shake.

I got out and fell on the ground crying. I could see those two huge trees; with the branches lying all over the surrounding ground. Oh God; there was broken glass strewn everywhere.

My tears fell hard; as I gathered up Patrick's things; they had flown out of the back of his truck on impact.

Oh Lord' "There is one of my son's golf shoes;" "I just bought him those new shoes not two weeks ago."

Oh Patty; there are your treasured golf tees all over the ground mixed in with all the broken glass and blood! Broken CD's were strewn everywhere. Later I thought; CD's are virtually indestructible; not in this horrible accident!

Everyone was in shock and crying out of control.

My nephew took my hand and walked me back along the roadway.

He wanted to show me where the vehicle had left the roadway.

My son's truck left the roadway with the passenger tires for quite a distance.

Later thinking about the opinion; that he either 'passed out' or 'feel asleep' and the distance the truck traveled; 'straight as an arrow' did not come together for me mentally? The truck in the darkness of the night and the remote highway; hit a drainage culvert that went under a driveway.

Hitting this culvert caused My Son's truck to go 'airborne.'

Airborne! Those darn over-sized tires on his truck!

The truck flew over the top of a building; hit two, huge 'trees head on'. It came to rest standing up on its side.

Landing on the driver's side—which was, I believe; Patrick's position. From the look of the totaled out truck; who can really say which young man was driving?

Terrified, drunken teenagers are capable of saying and doing anything!

We were on the way back to what used to be 'home.'

Along the way; I noticed a group of my son's friends; standing in front of a garage.

I had to argue with my Sister as I wanted her to stop; I had to talk with these young men!

I got out; trembling, shaking, and crying hard.

I asked them; "What happened to Patrick?"

None of them would look up from the ground.

They all were doing the same weird thing with their feet!

The same strange shuffling of their feet in the ground; as the teenagers who came to the house were doing. "Body Language" tells many things!

Staring at the ground and slowly moving their feet; back and forth, sideways in the soil!

They did not 'owe up' to being with My Son that night.

I later found out they had been with Patrick.

The young women that came immediately to the house were with Patty too; also; some of the other young men who came to the house right away!

I learned they had all left this Distant Community together; vehicles traveling in 'unison' back out to where they lived.

CHAPTER 16

A BIG PART OF ME; WANTED TO

BE ALONE

Returning to the house; I recall many people being there. Between the people coming and going; and the telephone ringing; it was too overwhelming for me!

'A Big Part' of me; wanted to be ALONE!

Patrick's Father arrived; this was the first time we had spoken and hugged each other since 1994.

Two completely broken, shattered people holding each other and crying, trembling and shaking!

WHY? "WHY; JESUS WHY?"

We all went into the house for a short time. I saw my ex glancing around our home with his eyes. I sensed he could not 'handle' being there.

I told him; "We waited for you to be here;" "We are going to the hospital to see Patty." "Would you like to come with us?"

He agreed; we went in two different vehicles; stopped for my second time at the scene of the horrible, tragic accident that claimed the 'lives' of two Beautiful Young Men! This was the first time Patrick's Father had been to the accident scene.

Everyone; made a 'big mistake' when they allowed me to go into the Pharmacy alone. My treating physician had called a prescription into the pharmacy for me; he was worried about me.

I could hardly walk in there; when I did; the tears came so hard and fast!

The women there were kind and understanding. They hugged me tight; gave me tissues and walked me to the door.

Patrick's girl was there in the vehicle waiting for me.

She held My Hand; the rest of the way; through it all. She kept 'her eye' on me and did not leave me alone. Patrick's girl is a completely, beautiful young woman.

Highly intelligent and religious. A Beautiful young woman; both inside and out.

My Son's Love and His Mother held hands and walked slowly into the hospital.

The rest were there; with us.

We sat in a waiting room for awhile.

My ex had; his soon to be new wife; with him.

My Daughter; Granddaughter and Son In Law would not arrive until the following day.

Out of "Love" for My Son; I let many statements from my ex husband and his gal go right by me. I could have picked up on their 'baited remarks'; I chose to keep my lips 'zippered.'

My son's girl and I were first in line; heading to see Patty!

We held hands; tight.

Back at the house; I was finishing another phone conversation when she approached me.

In a quiet, sad, small voice she said; "Can I stay with you please?" "Can I go to the hospital with you?"

As I hugged her I cried and said 'Yes; this is going to be incredibly difficult."

"Are you certain you can handle it?"

She wanted to see and 'lay claim' to the 'Young Man She Loved.'

I know now; she wanted to take back; take back; what she considered to be her's; Patrick!

She and I; were the first to enter the 'cold room.'

They pulled Patrick out on a steel table.

We looked at each other; held hands; cried and walked forward.

There was OUR PATRICK; his head was wrapped well in bandages; a sheet was over his body; his flesh was embedded with fragments of glass.

Oh God! This had to be the most painful time in my life.

Not too long before; My Beautiful Son was filled with Life and a Pure Love for people. His handsome face was smiling and laughing as he looked at me.

Oh "Jesus" Look at My Beautiful Son now!

Each took their turns walking up to see their Beloved Patty.

155

As we were walking down the hallway; I stopped; I knew I had to see My Son a second time.

The nurses needed a 'few minutes.'

My son's girl and I walked hand and hand back in the room.

I had to take a long hard 'look' at My Son's Face.

If Patty had suffered greatly with pain; fright and terror; this would show in His Face.

"All would show in His Face.'

It was NOT in His Face.

Instead; My Son looked like he always did.

156

Like He did; when I would look into his room at night; standing there and watching him sleep.

Patrick held the same; at peace; "Look at me Ma," "I'm sleeping."

Months later; I thought of how his truck looked; and I remembered His Face in the hospital; I really began to wonder?

Back at the house; there were all Patty's friends from the Island. Patrick was not with his, 'normal crowd' that night and early morning of the tragedy.

His Friends from the Island were 'torn into pieces.'

More and more people arrived.

My son had many, many friends; not only from school; from everywhere!

Basketball; Golf and His Personality 'won' him many friends of all ages.

I told all the 'kids'; you can go into Patty's room; I do not even 'mind' if you put on some of your 'head banging' music—not all this time. In fact; I would like it; if you did. They did not!

I went into Patty's room and told all of the young people to take any clothing, CD's; small items that belonged to My Son. Items to have and 'hold'; of their Dear Friend's throughout their lives. All of the young people; except for two; entered Patrick's room.

Later on; Friends of Patrick's that were out of the area; at the time of the accident; came to see me. I allowed them the same quiet time in My Son's room and they also wanted many items of Patty's.

I was getting close to exhaustion. There was something else I had to do—and do; right away!

I had my neighbor take me to see the "Other Mother."

Another first on my list of the most painful things I have ever had to do!

I saw her as I walked into the room.

Sitting on the couch; in shock; crying so hard, her eyes were all swollen like mine.

We held each other in a rocking fashion and cried.

I told her where I was returning from.

Her mood changed; she wanted to know "Did You See My Son?"

I answered; "No."

She said to me; "Well, why not?" "You saw Your Son, why not mine?"

I answered; "It would not have been appropriate; the hospital would not have allowed it."

I am not certain; I think she could not handle seeing Her Son.

I grieve 'greatly' over the loss of both young men; not only My Son; His Friend Too!

We left and I spent the night at my neighbors.

He seemed to think I could just 'go to sleep.'

I tried; the tears would not stop; the shaking was not as extreme now.

I lay their crying; thinking of My Beautiful Son and wondering; "Oh Patty; how could this have happened to you?" "Happened to You and Your Friend?"

I wondered over and over again; who provided the alcohol to My Son and His Friend?

"Who bought the beer for you that Friday night?"

"Who provided the booze?" "Who is 'out there' right now; with a heavy, guilty conscience?" "That is' if they have one?"

Around four in the morning on Sunday I sat at the kitchen table.

With 3x5 note cards; through heavy tears; I wrote My Son Patrick's Obituary.

I wear reading glasses; my tears fell so heavy; my glasses kept coming off.

I needed to wipe them; I had to see!

As I wrote his Obituary; my mind was 'flooded' with the most beautiful, happy

163

memories of me and My Son and all the precious moments we shared together.

Thursday of this week; My Son was in the newspaper for his 'golfing skills and abilities.' All over the news on Saturday and Sunday they were announcing 'His Death.'

I read about My Son in the newspaper on Thursday and again the following Monday. Monday was his obituary!

CHAPTER 17

SUNDAY MORNING CAME

Sunday morning came; I did not sleep at all on Saturday night.

How can you sleep with tears falling so hard and heavy?

My neighbor and I went to the house and chose clothing and other items for My Son. I will never know where I gained the strength to do all the things I had to do?

I picked out golfing clothing for Patrick; small items; such as his favorite necklace, his prayer book, My Rosary, a Watch that belonged to his Grandpa, his favorite 'Beany Baby Dog.' Later; many other things were given to Patty for 'his journey' to the other side.

My neighbor drove me into the Distant Community where My Son had been on that Friday night and Saturday morning. We met my ex-husband and his new gal there. We met them at the Funeral Home; this was the nearest one.

We had to make the arrangements for Our Son's funeral.

I cried so hard; I knew My Son was there; Patty was there in the building.

The funeral director called me on Saturday night and told me he had My Son with him. Oh God; this is the most horrible pain!

167

I never had to plan a funeral in my life. Someone helped me; this help came from a 'power' greater than me.

I arranged everything; my ex chose the Remembrance Cards and the accompanying Thank You notes.

We did everything upstairs; it was time to go downstairs and choose what Our Son was to 'rest' in. My ex husband was wonderful; damn; it was so hard to do! He came up to me and said" If this is what you want; this is what you shall have." I looked at him through hard tears;

I caught his eyes; he quickly turned away, as his eyes were swollen with hard tears too.

Laying Your Child to 'rest' has to be the greatest pain anyone can feel in their lifetime. It is not 'natural'. Children are supposed to outlive their parents.

I hardly remember the drive back to what used to be 'home.'

As we arrived there, people were all over; outside and inside the house.

The 'kids' were all back. Family were also there when we arrived. A collection of photos of Patrick's were beautifully created on a remembrance photo board. I did not do this; My Son's true friends did. My nephew's girlfriend created a photo memory book. My nephew and some of the young men; along with my neighbor; created a beautiful board where they mounted all of Patrick's track medals; high school plaques and written in letters on the top; it said;

"Forever: In Our Hearts."

My daughter, Son In Law, and Granddaughter arrived. My daughter screamed in pain and grief when she got out of the car at the house. I held her and we cried and cried and cried together. Mom she said; "This is so unfair and wrong"; "Patrick; was just getting to the age where we could relate to each other." "Mom, My Little Brother was too responsible for this to have happened."

"Oh Mom'; how are we ever going to live and find any degree of happiness again?"

I held her and cried; I answered; "I wish I could answer you; I don't think we will ever be happy or smile again"; "not for quite sometime."

All day Sunday people came and went; many stayed. My son's love was there for me all the way through.

Aurora Borealis

The phone rang constantly and once again I felt exhausted; weak; drained and my tears and grief I knew; were only beginning.

Inside me I sensed; I would cry and grieve for the rest of my days on the earth.

There was much activity at the house on Saturday and Sunday—into Monday.

I asked 'the kids' if they would come up with a song that Patrick really 'loved.'

I told them to take their time; give this some thought.

I was out in the yard hugging and crying with people; they came out and gave me an answer. "The Dance" by Garth Brooks.

'He Belonged to Us'

On Monday my neighbor drove me and My Son's girl into the larger city.

We went in to see Patty's truck! I almost passed out! The tears; I could hardly see it; I knew I had to.

My Son's truck was damaged badly; the only thing left of it; were the two back tires!

I attempted to get into the cab of the truck. Everyone hollered at me; 'Stop.'

"You will get all cut up.'

Tears kept falling as I looked into the cab.

Broken glass everywhere; the truck was close to being crushed in all directions.

I wanted to retrieve Patty's cell phone and watch.

173

Aurora Borealis

I did not find any of these items.

As I cried; I had an outburst of temper. I cussed and threw crushed beer cans out of the cab of the truck. I did notice two beer boxes in the front of My Son's truck. Two thirty pac beer boxes!

There were empty 'pixie sticks' everywhere too.

In the cab I found one item; I still look at every day.

This is a purple beaded necklace; Patrick, hung it on his rear-view mirror and for a long time he wore it. This necklace held a 'special' meaning to him; unknown to me!

174

I cried hard as I looked in the back of the truck and found My Son's lunchbox cooler. Only a couple of nights before; I was happy; making his lunch and putting it in this cooler. "Oh Jesus: what happened to my son?"

I retrieved his golf clubs; golf bag and golfing umbrella; and the other missing golf shoe.

The golf clubs were to be given to Patrick's good friend; our neighbor.

The man; who taught Patty about the game of golf.

All; but one of the golf clubs were his; he chose one special golf club; cleaned and shined it and went into the larger City and bought some of Patrick's 'special' golf balls.

On the drive back to our living area; I had my neighbor stop at the funeral home.

I had to see My Beautiful, Young Son again.

This is hard to explain; it gave me some minute degree of comfort.

The funeral director was kind to me. He took me into the room where Patrick was in an 'everlasting sleep.'

The funeral director wanted Patrick's casket closed; he told us this right away.

I made the decision to have the casket 'open.'

I gave this decision serious thought; I told him; "No fix Patty up; as well as you can."

I wanted all the young people that came to see their friend—to remember Patrick as he was; to see him as he was now!

If it 'sunk' into one brain and saved one young life; it would be worthwhile!

I was able to get a few hours sleep on Monday night!

CHAPTER 18

TUESDAY ARRIVED

Tuesday arrived; this was going to be an incredibly painful, sad day.

This was becoming harder and harder on me.

My neighbor and I attended; the visitation for My Son's Friend.

As we walked up the steps of the church; my legs trembled and my body shook, hard. I could not 'stop' crying and grieving.

Not just My Son; another Mother's Son too!

Many people reached out and held me; we cried together.

I was trying to be strong; my strength had always come from My Son.

My Son was gone; he took 'my strength' with him.

Walking Up to the "Other Mother; will forever be on my list as 'one' of the most emotionally charged moments in my life.

They say, "Your Son, was driving to me"

These words were haunting my mind as I approached her.

We held each other and cried, I whispered; "I am so very, very sorry;" "OH JESUS, Why Our Sons?"

The rest of Tuesday we all spent; many of us, planning for Patrick's farewell.

Planning for Patrick's farewell; seeing his smiling, happy face in our thoughts and minds; grieving and crying.

Wednesday came and my neighbor and I attended the first funeral service.

Patrick's friend.

I believe; I cried Harder and Longer for Patrick's friend.

Inside of me; I cried and grieved greatly—two beautiful young men with promising young lives ' were taken from their loved ones; while their loved ones slept. "How Cruel Can Life Be?"

As I left the Other Mother, I remembered.

The thoughts entered My Mind again!

In May; my neighbor and I attended another local teenager's funeral.

He too; was taken!

He was killed in another horrible accident; in a different kind of way.

A sadness began to overcome me there. As I sat there and thought of his tender young age of fourteen; I cried harder than anyone present.

I cried harder; as the fourteen year old's friends carried him down the aisle.

I realized; they were the other basketball players on his team.

My mind traveled to Patrick's basketball days; the strangest feeling came over me. This was a powerful scary feeling!

I tried to avert my eyes; it was then the flower arrangements; one in particular; caught my eye.

I cried harder as I saw the 'basketball flower arrangement.'

Again this made me think of MY SON.

I returned home sad; that early afternoon.

A friend arrived unexpectedly; He asked me 'hey come on fishing with me;' 'it will cheer you up.'

We took my son's dog with us for the first time.

As we fished; I told him the story of the young boy and his funeral.

Despite my apparent sadness; we enjoyed the day.

Getting back to the house; Patrick was there. My fishing friend and I were happy to see Patty.

I was in the kitchen heading towards the door; Patrick and my friend were outside the door talking.

I remember walking out the door; reaching out and grabbing My Son. I held him very tight and cried.

I looked at Patrick and said "OH please Patrick;" don't ever let anything like that happen to you." "Patty; I could not handle it!"

My friend turned; looked at Patrick and said; 'did you hear what Your Mother said to you?" "Did you hear her cry Patty?"

My son looked deeply into both 'our eyes' with 'his own eyes' filled with tears and said; "No Ma," "I promise, I will NEVER do this to you."

This fishing friend came to see me a short time after My Son's Tragic accident. He remembered all too well; his conversation with Patrick; and what transpired with me over the other boys basketball team; the flower arrangement with the basketball in the center.

Remembering it all, he asked me; "What really happened to Patrick?"

This was to be a grueling time period for me. Grueling, incredibly painful and intensely sad!

We left My Son's friend's funeral and went straight to the Funeral Home where My Patrick lay!

CHAPTER 19

ONE FOOT IN FRONT OF THE

OTHER

Once again; my neighbor and good friend drove me to the Funeral Home in the Community where My Son had spent his last hours on this earth.

Bravely; I walked forward; one foot in front of the other; to see My Beautiful Son laying there at peace.

The funeral director was busy arranging all the plants and flowers that were sent to My Son.

My Neighbor and some of the family members set up various items too.

On a small table they placed Patty's basketball and his basketball trophies.

They placed the photo album; my nephew's girlfriend created; on the small table.

The funeral director found us an easel; on this they positioned the board with all the medals and plaques.

Another one was found; for the photo gallery that Patrick's friends had created for him at the house on Sunday.

I placed extra graduation photos of Patty next to the guest book and his Remembrance Cards. These photos were taken in August of 2000 and this was the beginning of August

2001. These photos, there were many; were gone in 'no time at all!'

Visitation hours for Patty were held in the afternoon and the evening.

All his family were there for him. All his friends arrived at various times; throughout the visitation.

I have never seen as many people at a visitation in my entire life.

I stood there and tried to greet each and every one of them. This was impossible; there were far too many teenagers and adults there.

I knew my ex husband would not be much of a help; he did not know these people. In all honesty; I only knew some; most I did not!

The visitation hours in the evening became even more hectic. People were lined up in front of the funeral home; all along the sideway and into the parking lot.

Patrick was very, well known and greatly loved.

I have been to visitations before; this one for My Son was different. People came; however; they did not leave. The young people and all the adults sat there and stayed until the visitation hours were over.

Many, many tears fell over the loss of Patrick. I am certain many of these tears were for Patrick's Friend too!

If Tears could build a stairway to 'heaven'; more than one stairway would have been built to reach up for Patrick and His Friend.

I greeted as many people as I could. I watched as groups of teenagers arrived.

They signed the guest book; stood there in the line; crying and slowly working their way up; to see what they remembered to be; their smiling, happy, loving, fun-filled friend.

193

Aurora Borealis

What they remembered only a few days earlier and what they saw were two different things altogether.

I honestly believe the loss of Patrick did have a strong impact on some of the teenagers. I can only pray the impact was great enough; upon their minds; to cause them to think about' underage drinking' and those who are only too willing to ' provide;' and allow the minors to get in a vehicle and drive away!

I saw one woman in her forties come into the funeral home that evening.

I did not know her name.

I remember seeing her at a grocery store in a near by town.

I recall what she had said to me three times about My Son.

As I was going through the check out; she would ask; "How Is Pat doing?"

Being an honest person I would say" I am having trouble with My Son; someone is buying beer for him." "I keep sitting him down and talking with him about this' underage drinking."

She replied; "OH yes; I have seen Pat drunk before." One day at this store, she said to me; "Your Son is drinking too much!"

195

She hugged me at the funeral home that Wednesday evening; she was crying uncontrollably!

We spoke briefly and I noticed she had a hard time approaching Patrick.

Later after reading some State Police Reports and Investigative Reports; I learned this women; the woman who made these statements about MY SON; was buying and providing alcohol to Patrick and his friends; for quite some time before his accident. She was one of the alcohol providers!

How could she make these statements to me in the grocery store; and have the 'nerve' to show up at My Son's funeral; all along knowing she contributed greatly to the deaths of Patrick and his friend?

Her name came up as the' suspect alcohol provider' for both of the young men on their last Friday Night.

Another thing I heard; that caused me to stop and wonder; was two, different women at the funeral home; what they said to me and My Daughter.

As one woman; I did not know; hugged me, she said; "He Belonged To Us!"

Through my grief and tears this statement haunted me and caused me to really wonder?

Another woman, My Daughter did not know; hugged her and said, "He Was One Of Us!"

My daughter and I later discussed these comments.

Patrick was his own person; he was 'our flesh and blood.' He did not belong to them. I gave birth to this Beautiful Young Man; Patrick Belonged To Us and to "Jesus."

How twisted was the thinking of these 'clannish' backwoods people?

Before the visitation hours ended; I spoke with the funeral director.

I asked him "Is it possible; tomorrow at the Church; to leave Patrick's casket open for about 10 minutes." This was to allow his friends to place one small item in with Patrick; to travel with him to his 'New Home.'

The funeral director was reluctant to begin with.

He explained to me Patty had heavy cosmetics on; he feared it would start to fade with the heat and humidity.

He agreed to my request.

Before everyone left the funeral home on Wednesday night; I announced this to all the young people.

This gave them a small degree of happiness; they all wanted a part of themselves to 'travel' on with their Beloved Friend!

CHAPTER 20

MY BEAUTIFUL BABY BOY

I managed to sleep for a few hours on Wednesday night.

I awoke and the tears; grief and tremendous pain were still with me.

This was Thursday; 'OH Jesus' "Be with me today."

This morning is my Patrick's funeral.

As I got out of my neighbor's car; my legs began to fail me.

I could hardly move them; to walk up the stairs and into the church.

Once again; help came from a source unknown to me.

'He Belonged to Us'

I walked up to my Beautiful Baby Boy; I cried hard and deep. I reached out and touched his beautiful, long eyelashes and his little chin whiskers. Patrick was so proud of his chin whiskers; I always wanted those long eyelashes for myself.

I touched my lips with my finger and placed a kiss on his lips.

I felt so sick and wrong inside!

How could this have happened to My Son. He was highly intelligent—destined to be something great in life!

No! Not anymore. Not in his life upon the earth!

There were individuals at the funeral and Mass; sitting there; knowing they had undermined everything; My Son and I set out to achieve. To, achieve for Patrick. They had undermined me all the way and look; look where My Beautiful Son was now!

The pain and tears were overwhelming. I felt sick and wrong inside!

The funeral director obliged me. Sitting in the front row with family; I watched as many teenagers; friends of Patty's walked up to him crying and shaking. They all placed small objects in with their friend.

The funeral director closed the casket and

"God" this has to be the worse pain 'A Mother'

can ever feel. Nothing in my life; ever again;

would come anywhere close to this pain. I

knew it!

There was a beautiful Funeral Mass and a

'special friend' of mine and Patrick's; with her

clear voice did all the singing. What a

wonderful woman!

I cried and cried as everyone in the church

did!

I had given my son's boss; permission to

get up and speak.

Oh yes; he spoke. Did, he ever!

My son's boss was an Ordained Minister.

Patrick would always tell me, "Ma, I carefully choose the clothes I wear to work."

"I, carefully think before I speak at work Ma."

"My boss and owner of the business, is a very religious man."

"I love my work Ma; everything about it."

"I, respect my boss Ma" for his beliefs in Jesus and the man that he is!"

Patrick's boss spoke loud and clear.

He had been in this area for about the same time period as My Son and I.

He came down real heavy on what he had seen since living here!

He brought up the subject of 'underage drinking' and those who are only too willing to provide. He spoke 'highly' of Patrick.

He said' Patrick was so smart; so highly intelligent."

"Patrick; could have been anything he wanted to be in life."

"Look where he is now!"

"What happened to Patrick?"

One of My Son's friends got up and spoke beautifully about Patty. He was the chosen spokesman for all the young people.

207

Next My Daughter; Patrick's Sister got up and spoke through heavy tears.

My Granddaughter spoke about her Uncle; through heavy tears.

My neighbor walked up; what he said about Patrick was beautiful.

I am not a public speaker; too shy and timid!

I will never know how; I gathered the necessary strength; to get up looking into a huge crowd of people. They were everywhere; leaning against the walls, in the small room where you entered the Church; down the wide

long stairs and out all along the sidewalk.

It was my body and my mouth standing

there speaking. This I know!

The words and thoughts came smoothly out

of my mouth. There was a 'power' greater than

me; choosing the thoughts and the words.

I was standing there looking at all these

people; it was my body and my mouth; but

someone else was speaking for Patrick!

Towards the end of my words about My

Son; I announced "The Special Song" that the

'kids' chose for Patty.

Aurora Borealis

The song they had chosen; "The Dance" by Garth Brooks was played repeatedly; as all of my son's pall bearers carried Patty out of the church.

My son's best friend; from the Island; chose the pall bearers.

Earlier; My Son's neighborhood friend had taken my hand; together we walked up; placed Patrick's favorite golf club and golf balls in the casket with him.

Many of the older men Patrick golfed with did the same; before Patrick was closed in his casket. They all came and placed a sleeve of golf balls in with their young golfing 'buddy.'

They all cried so long and hard!

All of these men, one by one, looked at me and said the same words.

"I just saw Patrick this week; I golfed with him."

"What happened to Patrick?"

"The Dance played over and over again as Patrick and everyone left the church for the drive to his' final resting place."

There was not a 'dry eye' to be seen. Many, many people grieved greatly over the tragic loss of My Son and his friend.

A tragic loss that should never have happened!

Two, Beautiful, intelligent, young men with bright promising lives were gone!

The consumption of Alcohol in this Backwoods location was too accepted as being the 'norm.' Generation after generation, thought this was the only way to live—life!

CHAPTER 21

TEARS FROM HEAVEN

I watched as My Son was placed in the Hearse.

My eyes hurt badly from the heavy tears that fell.

I trembled and shook; my legs would hardly stand!

My insides felt so sick.

My grief was almost unbearable!

We waited in cars; behind the vehicle; Patrick would take his last ride in!

When we went into the church; the skies were blue; still, it was an incredibly hot, humid day.

When we exited the Church the skies were the same way.

Leaving the village, we drove down the road; right by the house; My Son And I once called 'home.'

My tears fell harder.

Just as we left our road and turned onto' the highway;' where this horrible accident took place; the skies changed rapidly.

From out of no-where; a wild Summer storm came; we all drove right into the storm.

The rain was heavy; driven by strong winds. As we drove; the trees were whipping down towards the ground from the force of the powerful winds.

Driving was incredibly hard. The drivers could hardly see; needed their headlights on; the skies were that black. There was loud thunder and tremendous, lightening strikes all around us!

We drove and rode through this; all the way to Patrick's 'resting place.'

Arriving at the Chapel, it began to let up; there was still the loud thunder and the lightening strikes.

In the Chapel ' Final Words' were spoken.

We left the chapel to place Patty in the ground.

The cemetery workers did not want to do this; not at this time.

Not with the lightening strikes!

The funeral director understood me when I said; "No, I have to know where My Son is." "I will never be able to sleep, until I know."

Once again he obliged me; along with the help of one of his employees.

Many stood around weak with tears and grief. Stood there; watched as they lowered My Beautiful Baby Boy into the ground! "Oh

217

Jesus," This is the worse pain, a Mother can ever endure.

Afterwards; I rode silently back out our way with my neighbor.

All I did was cry and cry and cry.

My Tears would not stop!

My Son was gone from me' physically'; Forever!

'Spiritually'; He would Live On "Within Me." Forever!

Patrick was so 'deep' in my heart, my mind and my soul!

I thought to Myself; 'This was the most dreadful mistake of my life.'

"I should NEVER have taken My young, impressionable Son into this backwoods, 'clannish' location of Northern Michigan.

The people were too 'regional' and 'clannish.'

'Alcohol' was too accepted as being the normal way to live one's life.

Generation after generation after generation grew up and lived this way.

An older Uncle of mine; called me later; he told me something I did not know and will never forget about 'Life and Death.'

219

The violent weather; came out of 'no where' and lasted throughout the drive to the Chapel; was called "Tears From Heaven."

He said to me; "I am an old man; I have only seen this happen once before in my long life.

"Tears From Heaven.' "Heaven was crying for Patrick!"

CHAPTER 22

ONCE CALLED HOME

I stayed with my neighbor; my good friend afterward.

I now, found myself still crying, grieving internally and outwardly.

There were many details I had to 'close out.'

It is painful enough to lose Your Son; whom, you Loved deeply; all the paperwork afterwards was overwhelming! Slowly, I worked on it all, slowly; it was taken care of and completed.

My neighbor and I returned to the house; My Son and I once called 'home.'

At some point; on the Monday after the accident the storm door which led into our kitchen; had been 'kicked in.'

We went shopping and purchased another door.

My son's last paycheck paid for the new door.

I mentioned this to the State Trooper; he was not interested!

He said to me; "It's too late now!"

I asked him; "Don't you want to see the kicked in door?"

He replied; "No."

The kicked in storm door; in my mind; would have been evidence.

My Son's truck and its contents; would have been evidence too!

I called the Company who had My Son's truck. I spoke with the owner; told him about My Investigator wanting to see the truck. He agreed to not destroy the truck or the contents. When My Investigator arrived at the company; the owner became angry! He said My Son's Insurance Company had called him.

They told him to crush the truck 'as soon as possible.'

The storm door, the truck and its contents were all evidence.

All; except the storm door were gone forever!

As he worked on the door; I cleaned the house and began the painful process of going through Patrick's clothing.

I went through each item of clothing; slowly with Love and Tears!

As I looked at each item; I knew who to give each piece of clothing to.

The other clothing went to the Church the annual Summer 'fund raising sale.'

Aurora Borealis

The day came for me, when I knew inside of me; it was time to go to the house alone.

This was a horrible feeling.

Everything I looked at; reminded me of Patrick!

Everything!

There was Patty's dog and his little Bird.

The little bird faired well; she was her normal perky self.

My Son's dog ; on the other hand; was not himself.

When he heard a noisy vehicle; he would run to the door howling and crying.

He would sit there howling and patiently waiting.

Waiting for 'someone' that was NEVER going to walk through that door again.

The dog's sadness only increased my grief and pain.

One night, I was in the living room when My Son's dog began acting 'out of character.'

He was in the middle room; growling into Patrick's bedroom; growling and leaping back as if in 'fear.'

He spooked me!

I tried to calm the dog down; I was not successful.

Finally; I carried him into My Son's room; held him there where He and Patty spent many happy fun-filled hours together.

I petted him, tried to 'calm' him down.

He leaped out of my arms and NEVER entered 'His Boy's room again.

Quickly; I found Patrick's dog; an excellent home in the country with an old High school friend.

My Son's dog loves his 'new life' and is able to run free.

A happy, frisky dog now!

I began to enter Patrick's room more and more.

On one day; I went through everything; I threw some items away.

I carefully arranged his room in a 'beautiful' way!

On another day; I decided this 'hurt' too much.

I went through everything again; giving many more things away to MY Son's close friends.

Lovingly; I sorted through everything and purchased dark green trunks.

229

Within these trunks, I placed everything that was to be kept.

I went through the house and took every 'photo' from My Life; also packing them away in the trunks. I could not look at a picture of MY Beautiful Son at this time; the pain was too intense!

My Son's books were donated to a larger City; to a Catholic elementary school.

Also, his 'treasured' movies. Most of mine were donated in His Memory too.

We watched these movies together; the thought of watching them without MY Son hurt!

The School sent me many notes; telling me, "Your Son's legacy shall live on."

I received another note when the school children watched a movie My Son had; 'Joan of Arc.' 'Joan of Arc' died at the age of 19 too!

The school called me throughout the fall, the winter and into the spring. The ladies would talk to me for an hour, they cared, wanted to know how I was doing?

I donated money to this school for their annual renovation fund raiser.

Donated this money; in memory of My Beautiful Son.

This will continue to be an annual tradition for me!

I held a small life insurance policy on My Son. This was started when Patty was three.

A week before his accident; I showed it to him.

I said; "Patrick, Real soon, you can convert this into whole life insurance."

"As you live your life, and ever get into a bind; you can borrow against this policy."

Saying these things to My Son; I had 'no' way of knowing he would Never reach this point in his life!

CHAPTER 23

THE DATE AND THE TIME

At the house; I found myself walking the floor.

The place was 'Never' going to be the same.

A few of the neighbors stopped in to see me; from time to time.

My Brother and a 'special aunt' called me.

Also; my lifelong friend from another State called me many times.

She made many calls to obtain my telephone number; finally she reached me.

Years earlier; I grieved with her over the loss of her own 14 year old son.

He also died in a horrible, tragic auto accident in another State.

She called crying; it took us awhile to gain enough control to speak.

If anyone knew the pain and grief I was enduring; it was my 'special' lifelong friend.

During the course of one of our conversations she told me "August 4th" was the day Her Son was born. August 4th" was the day I lost My Son.

Another strange occurrence is; My Son died at exactly the same time My Daughter was Born!

Later; I learned when I called A Good Friend in My Hometown; crying out of control; to tell him about Patty; August 4th was His Birthday. He did not tell me this until months later. With all my pain and grief; I had forgotten his Birthday for the first time in years!

The people from the Village and the surrounding areas; despite their words; did not attempt to see or call me.

I learned that words are only words; unless they are spoken seriously from 'the Heart.'

When things slowed down, I remembered the names of the young men and women that came to the house on that Saturday.

I wrote letters to both the Michigan State Police and the Prosecuting Attorney.

My letters wanted 'written statements' from all of these young people.

I also hired a Private Investigator for a brief time.

He tried and did get to speak with a few people.

He was immediately told'" Doesn't she know, 'she' is an 'outsider' to us."

They told him "she is too honest and upfront, honest to the point of being abrasive."

This Private Investigation ended quickly. How can you get the truth out of a group of 'clannish' people trying to 'protect' their own?

The Private Investigator wrote in his report' "This Village and its people are well known as being extremely clannish!"

"I know one young man; in particular is lying."

The State Police did their investigative work. The law was not happy with me; I was seriously searching for answers.

239

The State Trooper came to the house one day.

We sat at the table in the kitchen; I was still grieving greatly!

I had a photo of Patrick on the window shelf in the kitchen. His photo was with his Grandfather's photo. Along with the photos I had a Rosary. My Son had made me this wonderful window shelf in earlier years. He made it for all my house plants; he knew I loved to grow things. It was also made for his Little Bird to sit on during the day. She could then look outside see and hear the wild birds.

During our brief conversation; I did gaze over at My Son and Father a few times.

He thought I had mental issues and later wrote this in one of his reports.

What is wrong with looking at a photo of your son whom you loved completely?

He thought I needed psychiatric care!

Our conversation was short; he appeared to be in a hurry.

He told me things; he had discovered in his investigation; real fast.

He then looked at me and said; 'There! Now that you have answers" are you happy?"

He said this to me in a cold, cruel way!

241

My response was well Trooper; "At this point I am happy I hired a Private Investigator."

He promised me, if they could not get information on the alcohol provider; the law would run something on Crime Stoppers.

I waited and waited—nothing was on Crime Stoppers.

My decision came easy, I made some calls and forced this Trooper to keep his 'word.'

I heard it on the radio one morning and I fell on the floor; I laid there and had a long hard cry.

As time went by; I began to go places by myself. Some people were caring and they said to me; "What is the law waiting for?" "When are they going to do something about the deaths of the two boys?"

I did not have an answer for them!

I gave one man 'credit' for finding my son's truck and My Son and his friend.

One night at my house; I heard a door in the driveway slam.

I looked out and it was this man.

I was deeply involved in a mountain of paperwork; he came to the door.

I said "Hello" opened the door and let him in.

All I could smell was booze! He could hardly talk to me. He wanted to tell me something; but could not get it out.

Finally; I took control and said' Please Tell Me Why You Came Here?"

He then said; "I have to warn you"; 'let it go' 'you don't know what will happen to you if you don't."

He left; he had scared me during the time he was at my house.

Later; I learned I gave the wrong man credit for finding My Son's truck; My Son and his friend; the credit belonged to someone else. This man had taken the credit for something he did not do!

CHAPTER 24

CREATING THE MEMORIALS

I went alone to the Chapel Gardens where Patrick rested.

Time had passed and I began to worry about Patty's Memorial Stone.

As I drove there; my tears fell once again. I was driving the same highway; My Son had lost his life along.

Towards the end of this highway; I glanced over through my tears and saw two beautiful young horses galloping through the field.

Wild and Free!

My mind turned once again to My Son and His Friend.

247

The Horses reminded me of their two young lives.

At the Chapel; I sat at a table still shaking and crying.

This is where I created My Son's Memorial Stone.

My creation would take some time to achieve.

An artist had to make a sketch from one of Patty's graduation photos; this would be eventually etched into his stone at the top.

This was 'My Favorite' graduation photo.

A close up of Patrick's smiling, happy, young face with his beautiful teeth white and sparkling.

I chose a different color stone from all the others.

Also: a different type of print.

Under his etched in photo on one side was the day he entered the earth; the other side was the day he left the earth.

Next; his name.

Under his name I had these words placed in parenthesis.

"Shooting Star"

Under those words etched in the stone are a basketball player and a golfer.

The Memorial Stone arrived around the time of my Birthday in the fall of the year.

Once again I cried and drove to his 'resting place.'

I was there as they placed the stone in the ground.

The first time I went there by myself; my legs gave out.

I fell down on the ground crying and praying; right over My Son.

This was not an easy time, however; the placing of My Son's stone brought a small degree of happiness to My Heart.

I felt relief! The small plastic name plate; increased my grief; I did not want my Son; Patrick to be 'buried as a 'pauper.'

My ex husband; Patty's Father paid for all the funeral expenses and most of the Memorial Stone.

I am grateful to him for this; on my own; I don't know how I would have acquired this large sum of money.

My neighbor and I right away; began making two, beautiful memorial crosses.

Five foot high—solid oak—later painted with each young man's name.

Trailing flowers ran down each cross. An artist friend of his; did all the creative painting. I am eternally grateful to both of them; kind, caring men!

The crosses were sealed; and later a white fluorescent paint was put on the edges.

We placed the crosses within the state easement.

This day was very, very hard on me.

As we raked and cleared the area at the base of the large tree, I fell to the ground again!

Tears fell; I continued to work through them.

On the ground everywhere among the broken glass were golf tees.

These golf tees belonged to My Patrick; his hands touched these golf tees.

I gathered many of them; placing them in my pockets.

My Son's Memorial Cross later caused some problems; with the people who owned the wooden shed that was caved in by the accident.

253

They attempted to intimidate me into paying them a large sum of money for a modern, large, new garage.

I contacted My Attorney; fast as possible. He handled the situation; a large modern new garage was built. I have No Idea; who paid for it!

I sent them a letter; advised them that My Son's Cross was within the state easement and that it shall remain where it was lovingly placed. Lovingly placed where Patrick and His Friend had 'shed' their 'last blood.'

At night both of the boy's crosses can be seen a great distance away.

Head lights cause the crosses to 'glow.'

One evening in the late fall; while watching television, the phone rang.

I answered in my still sad voice "Hello"

I heard a man's voice on the other end; a man's voice disguised somehow.

He said the following to me;

"You better let it go"

"Keep quiet"

"Or YOU will go; the same way Your Son did!"

A couple night's later; I received the same threatening phone call.

Next came two different calls from a teenage male.

He asked; "Can I speak to Pat?"

My heart sank as I answered; "No, Patrick is not here any longer."

He let out a laugh and said; "Oh that's right"

"I forgot."

He hung up!

I had No Choice; I had to inform the law of these calls; they wanted me to put it in writing; I obliged them and mailed the letters out.

I immediately called my telephone company; they kindly changed my number to a new unpublished one; within about one half hour!

My Investigator wrote in his report that initially The State Trooper was cooperative. He abruptly changed!

I believed that the 'Other Mother' would choose to seek answers, the truth and justice such as I did.

I was completely wrong!

She conveyed 'Her Wishes' by way of the State Trooper to the Prosecuting Attorney.

She wanted any investigations stopped immediately!

She stated: "She could not begin healing until this was done."

I thought about this and realized I wanted answers, truth and justice.

She wanted to 'let it go.'

What about me?

How was the Law going to handle this situation?

Once again; after reading reports; I learned the 'Other Mother' was first cousins with the suspected alcohol provider on that Friday Night.

The same woman; who had 'fueled' My Son and other young men with alcohol throughout time.

I received a phone call from an old friend the day after Easter.

He had news for me; I later checked it out; it was true!

The suspected alcohol provider spent Easter Sunday in jail for 'fueling' a 16 year old male with alcohol and then sexually molesting him.

She got 'out' the following Tuesday.

I do not know the 'outcome' of this charge.

There was enough information in the First and Second State Police Reports for arrests to me made. It was proven this 'woman' provided alcohol to my Son's Friend on that Friday night; was she arrested for this? I tried to find out; and got 'no where.'

There were parties at private residences in this distant Community; parents allowed them to take place; were they arrested? No!

The Street dance was referred to as:' one very large traveling tail gate party; with people of all ages; all ages; openly consuming alcohol.'

Was this Community held accountable by the Law; were charges filed? NO!

There was one officer from the county positioned outside of this Community; He and the car were facing the opposite direction. This way he would not see what was transpiring in this Community!

I would much rather have received a phone call in the early morning hours.

A phone call telling my; My Son was in jail for Minor in Possession or Drunken Driving or

Driving Under the Influence. Anything else!

Instead of having; an Officer of the Law come

to our home and tell me this 'life devastating

news!"

I made another well thought out decision.

I decided to list my place on the market at

such a low price; it would sell real fast.

This came true for me.

I could No Longer stay in this; out of the

way Northwoods area' and ever live a 'Happy

Life.' I lived in fear of these 'clannish' people

and the calls I received!

I was invited one evening up my road to some neighbors for dinner.

I tried not to speak of Patty; this did not happen.

Patrick was spoken of; by this family.

Their older son was a good friend; he was the one who came down and watched movies and played cards with us; years earlier.

They told me about a graduation party they attended in 2001.

This party took place in the Village at a hall.

They were not there long; before they noticed the two long tables.

Seated at the two long tables were underage teenagers 'pouring' beer down rapidly!

They were so 'disgusted'; they walked out!

This graduation party took place during the daylight hours.

Parents sat there openly allowing this to happen.

Setting the example of; this is 'acceptable behavior.'

This Village does not 'heed the law'; they allow minors to enter two of the bars later at night and into the early morning hours. Why?

My Son asked me a few times to 'buy' him some beer.

My answer was the same 'No' 'No' "No"

"Vitamin K, Patrick."

"No"

Patrick would say to me; "well why not?'

My answer was always the same" If anything ever happened to you and anyone with you"; "I could not live with myself."

I attended Mass in the Village twice a week, however; this did not last long.

It became 'clear' to me I was not welcome there:' I was not 'one of them!'

Next; I attended Mass twice a week in a small neighboring community.

A few of the people there were kind to me.

When I realized that most would not reach out and take my hand; and say 'peace be with you'; I stopped attending Mass.

I thought these people were church going, good people; God Loving People.

Later; I drove a long distance and attended Mass in a much larger City.

CHAPTER 25

TRAVELING THE HIGHWAY

During my time living Up North; I traveled the highway My Son lost his life along.

As I traveled the highway; I began looking at this highway closer than ever before!

This highway at night was normally dark and desolate.

There are two other roads than run parallel to it.

These; two other roads have many side roads.

A person could easily come out on one of the other highways; take one of the crossroads and be 'right there' on the highway My Son and His Friend 'lost' their lives along.

As I drove the highway during the day; I would drive the entire distance.

While I drove I analyzed this highway!

If My Son had passed out at the wheel or fallen asleep; how did he make it around all the dangerous, dangerous sharp curves?

The area where His Truck left the roadway was on a 'lengthy', wide open stretch of the highway?

The more I traveled this highway; the more "My Maternal Instincts' told me; No, something is not right about the accident!

I read statements from the involved teenagers, State Police Reports, Investigative

269

Reports; I remembered what 'each and everyone' of them told me when they came to the house; and also speaking to them in front of the garage along the highway.

What they said did not make sense; their statements were not the same!

The puzzle pieces did not 'fit together.'

I believe My Son was forced off the road by another vehicle. Patrick, was not a 'fighter'; there was trouble that night between him and another young man—' a fight' over a young woman.

It is my understanding this fight did not last long!

When Patrick was driven off the road; I believe he thought he could continue on through the ditches; and eventually get off the road completely or back on to the road!

In the darkness of this desolate highway; He had 'No Way of Knowing' he would hit a drainage culvert and go airborne and this would be the end for him and his friend.

Patrick was drug tested spontaneously on the ferry; he did not do drugs.

Could someone have given him a drug such as GHB or Ecstasy in his beer without his knowing? A sick, drunken teenage joke; not thinking of the 'deadly' consequences?

I know My Son had freedom of choice.

He chose to go into that distant community for the Friday Night Street Dance.

He chose to consume some beer!

Patrick was not 'of age'; He could not walk into a store or a bar and 'legally' obtain alcohol for himself! Someone 'of age' provided it to him; not caring about the fact he might drive!

What he did not choose to do that early morning was his usual behavior.

Patrick; if he drank; would 'stay' where he was.

He knew better than to drive!

Why on this early Saturday morning did he change his normal behavior and patterns? Why did he choose to drive the great distance home?

I did some research and have documents to back up my statements.

My Son did not have any record, anywhere, with the law.

Patrick; also had a clean driving record; He did not have any records of wrong doing!

My Son was well known and well liked by so many people in all areas of Northern Michigan!

The State Police would not release any information on this accident to the newspapers who called them or the Television Stations. Why?

CHAPTER 26

DREAM VISITATIONS AND

STRANGE PHENOMENA

Aurora Borealis

Shortly after returning to my place in the Northwoods; I began having what I thought were dreams of Patrick.

My Son would come to me in my dreams; telling me things.

One morning after waking; I sat up in bed repeating two words over and over again.

I wrote these words down and remember them well.

The words came from Patty.

Right afterward, I went to; touch tone dial a neighbor.

I looked down and thought to Myself; "Now what the heck happened there?"

The phone numbers in this area all started with the first three numbers.

It was my finger reaching out to 'touch' the numbers.

My finger; not my response!

All of a sudden my finger moved off the numbers and on to three different ones.

I also recorded this strange occurrence.

There was another dream of My Son. In this dream he told me something about boots. This was also recorded.

Early one morning; I abruptly woke from my sleep.

277

I sat up; opened my eyes; there standing at the top of the stairs was Patrick.

While I was sleeping; My Son was watching me.

I closed my eyes; looked again; he was gone.

Right after I returned home; while laying on the couch in the living room; my eyes would catch a movement.

This movement was shadowy and came from My Son's Room.

I was not the only one that witnessed this shadowy movement.

A friend came out to see me one night after work; I was gone at the time.

He came in and while waiting for me; fell asleep on the couch.

Returning home: I found him there; as I woke him; he was greatly startled.

It was then; he told me about the shadowy movement; he saw coming from My Son's room.

The shadowy movement was only there for a short time.

Then it disappeared and 'Never' came back.

One night; I returned from a larger City. Before leaving, I stopped and bought some roastbeef sandwiches and placed them in the refrigerator. All this time I was thinking of Patty.

Patty loved them so much!

When I would go into the distant City previously; the minute I came through the door I would hear: "Did you buy anything?' "Yes; I did Patrick look in the refrigerator."

On this particular night I went to the refrigerator, later, to get one of the sandwiches.

As I turned; I bumped right into the shadowy movement.

I did not know what to do or think?

I went into the living room; sat there eating my roast beef sandwich.

Many of these strange occurrences happened to me.

The most amazing; was with the green grape.

Patty and I both loved fresh, sour, green grapes.

It was a winter's day; standing by the kitchen cupboard; I went to pull one small bunch of the grapes off the larger bunch.

Grapes went flying; as I bent down, I complained out loud about winter and being so arthritic.

As I came up; I knew one of the grapes had rolled behind the coffeemaker.

I had the bowl for the grapes; placed beside the coffeemaker.

I reached towards the coffeemaker to pull it out; and retrieve the grape.

What happened next caused me to stand back and really wonder?

I did not get a chance to even touch the coffeemaker. About an inch high off the counter; this is what happened.

Smooth as can be like a curved 'three point shot" in basketball; the grape flew from around the back of the coffeemaker and landed 'directly' in the center of the bowl.

I ate the green grapes and decided to go to the neighbors and play some cards.

Time to get some fresh, cold air and out of the house!

I had one terrifying dream after My Son's death. My body was the same; as in all the terrifying nightmares; I had experienced previous to his death.

I woke up sweating, shaking and trembling. I was not crying; I was screaming; screaming "Devils," 'Get Away."

My son was in this dream; along with the young woman he was with; on that tragic Friday night and Saturday Morning. There were Devils and there also was a drug called Ecstacy!

This nightmare was also recorded and I could not shake this 'strange' feeling throughout my entire being! This feeling stayed with me through the entire day and night!

I stood back; did not know what to think about all this.

It was then; I called My Daughter and began to tell her of these strange occurrences.

My Daughter reported: she also saw Her Little Brother; one day in her house.

She told me the story of her birthday and the sad, low mood that took over her body and mind.

There were errands to run; she left home and later returned.

My daughter went into My Granddaughter's bedroom to put some laundry away.

She could not believe her eyes or figure out how this happened.

There was' No Logical' explanation as to how a photo of her little brother when he was 'just' a little boy holding a birthday present: came to lay face up right in the center of her daughter's bed. Her husband was long gone into another City for work. She had taken My Granddaughter to school. 'The house' was locked with 'dogs in it.' One of these 'dogs' belonged to Her Patty; she talked him into giving her 'this dog.'

Many other unexplained phenomena have happened to both me and My daughter.

My Granddaughter also reports her Uncle coming to see her.

She is a young teenager and will not say much about his visits.

On the last visit; she said; "I asked Uncle' Pat' to be My Guardian Angel."

Both My Daughter and I have been reading many books on the subject of 'Death and Healing.' In the course of reading some of these books; we have learned about "The

Healing Power' of "After Death Communications."

The dreams are called "Dream Visitations."

The strange occurrences are called "Unexplained Phenomena."

CHAPTER 27

HAPPY NEWS TELEPHONE CALL

Aurora Borealis

Happy news came one day in the form of a telephone call.

There was a 'buyer' for my house in the Northwoods.

This gave me a sense of great 'relief."

It was lots of hard work; I sold it furnished.

Still; there were things the new owners did not want; a high school friend helped me; we found new homes for most everything.

I still had all the clearing out of drawers; cupboards etc.

Ah; how I dislike moving! Far too much work!

In my case; it was crucial.

While I was digging and sorting out everything; I found the beautiful birthstone tree.

I remembered that Christmas; like it was yesterday.

Patty was young; he had his own money; I took him Christmas shopping.

He spotted them in the store; and bought them.

He gave both me and His Father; that year; Beautiful, birthstone trees.

These trees were large trunked and Deciduous.

Finding this tree; now in my bedroom; caused me to cry once again.

I thought of the large trunked deciduous tree that' took' My Son from me.

The tool box holds a story too.

The tool box is something I open and use most everyday.

Around Mother's Day; in 2001; Patrick asked me a question.

"Ma; what do you want for Mother's Day this year?"

This was easy for me to answer; "A toolbox;" I said.

Patty repeated this to me; "A Toolbox?"

Mother's day came and My Son and I awoke.

He was happy as he went out to his truck.

Coming through the door, he said; "Close your eyes, Ma."

I closed them and opened them upon my son's command.

There on the table was a great toolbox. Just like the one I wanted.

In the toolbox was a Mother's Day card with $30.

Patrick made another trip to his truck.

Coming in; he reached out and gave me a Gorgeous Flower arrangement.

"Happy Mother's Day;" he said.

I reached out and hugged MY Son real tight and gave him 'the little smooch on the cheek'.

My wonderful Son was growing into such a fine young man.

This would be the last Mother's Day I would share with Patrick!

CHAPTER 28

THE AMAZING SIGHT

A couple of days; before leaving, what used to be "home," I saw something 'absolutely' amazing.

I was standing at the large kitchen window; the one facing the forest.

Just before the forest; My Son and I had created a large stone, ringed burning pit.

There as 'big as life' stood a Wolf!

I saw this 'wolf' the following evening too!

We had lived in this house for over 7 years together and not 'me' or My Son had ever seen a Wolf in our yard. We wished; none appeared. Patrick always possessed a Strong Love and Interest in 'Wolves.'

For years everything he wanted was connected with wolves!

The day came and I closed on the house.

There was one very important thing I had to do before driving out of Northern Michigan!

I went in 'person; to see the Prosecuting Attorney.

We spoke in his office for quite awhile.

I explained during the course of our conversation; "All I seek is Truth and Justice." "Nothing More."

We spoke of the horrible accident; the suspected alcohol provider and her later arrest.

297

He was very careful with his words and would not tell me much of anything.

He did tell me that the case was still very 'wide open.' He said; "It will remain open until I solve it."

I now sit back and wonder; "was he placating me or was he indeed serious?"

I drove out of Northern Michigan that night. Many times in my life I had driven out of Northern Michigan!

This was to be the hardest; saddest drive out 'of my life."

This time; only "ONLY ONE OF US" left!

298

I arrived; downstate late that night.

I was greeted by My Daughter; My Son In Law and My Beautiful Granddaughter. Greeted with tight hugs and kisses; great happiness and relief.

The following day My Daughter and I would drive away together.

She wanted to make certain Her Mother arrived 'safely' in her new living location.

CHAPTER 29

ALABAMA

THE ROBERT TRENT JONES

GOLF TRAILS

The following morning with a completely loaded car; filled with items that carried 'special meaning' to me; we drove away.

We were headed to my new residence.

Our relationship had been strained for quite sometime.

I 'sensed' My Son wanted us to reunite again.

To regain a 'Strong Mother-Daughter Love Bond.'

The first couple of days were tense; at times.

After that; it all came together.

We were close once again and I pray it remains this way!

My daughter did most of the driving—an excellent driver; she is!

As we drove; we talked and of course I looked around.

I burst into laughter; next tears as I saw a sign advertising a Motel.

I told My Daughter the following story.

Years back, when Patty was young I drove the two of us out West for a lengthy summer vacation.

Along the trip; he said to me with excitement; "Oh Look Mom," "That Motel Has suits!"

I looked over at the sign and with a smile I said to him;

"Oh Patty," "You are so cute."

He had just graduated from second grade.

The Motel had 'suites' however; to Patty the Motel had 'suits' there.

"Suits' for people to wear I assume?

On the second day of our trip; we were in Alabama.

As My daughter drove; I began to see 'Those Signs"

303

Aurora Borealis

I said to My Daughter, "Those are the Golf Courses they advertised Up North in the Winter Months;" "I promised Your Little Brother I would take him there golfing this year."

I cried; My Daughter Drove.

We stopped in the early afternoon in the State of Alabama.

Before dinner that late afternoon; we drove down a quiet, peaceful country road.

There was the sign; it was one of the "Robert Trent Jones Golf Trails."

The ones I had promised Patrick; I would take him to!

We parked the car; I reached in the glove box and found what I was looking for there.

We walked together on the Golf Trail and found a Beautiful huge Southern Pine.

Close to the tree; I pushed deep down in the ground—a golf tee from The Northern Golf Course where My Son worked and Loved to Golf. Patrick had touched this golf tee with his own hands!

We prayed together there under the tree; prayed and cried.

I said out loud after the prayers: "Patrick, Your Sister and I now have "Set Your Spirit Free;" "We have taken you back from the

Village People; taken you back in Spirit Patrick."

"Your Spirit is Free now; free to Golf forever; on one of the most Beautiful Golf Trails in the Country."

"Golf Baby, Golf!"

On the way to the restaurant for dinner, our eyes were heavy with tears.

We once again felt a strong, ever binding Mother and Daughter "Love."

We arrived safely at my new living destination. It is beautiful and exactly what I was praying for in my life.

306

Together; we managed to do a few fun things before her flight back to Michigan.

As we talked we grew closer and closer.

Two nights before My daughter's flight back to her home; she experienced a dream visitation from' Her Little Brother.'

She had fallen asleep that night; with Her Brother's blanket held tight to her body.

I awoke the next morning to her voice and the smell of coffee.

My daughter had coffee ready for Mom!

I thanked her; it was then she said this to me.

"Mom," "Patrick, came to me in my sleep last night."

I answered "Yes ; did he say anything?"

She answered "Yes."

"These are his exact words Mom" "Not Mine."

He said; "Listen to Ma" "There is more to 'my death' than what they're saying."

My daughter then said the name of a 'young woman'; there was NO Way she had any previous knowledge of this name.

She asked me who this' young woman' was and kept repeating her name.

I answered, "That is the name of the young woman;" "The young woman that was with Your Brother on that Friday night and early Saturday Morning." Patrick had told his Sister; this name over and over again in her sleep!

We looked at each other and sensed that My Son and Her Brother was trying to tell us things about "His Death."

We both knew from the beginning; there was more to Patrick's and His Friends Deaths!

CHAPTER 30

THE FIST

During one of our talks; My Daughter and I came upon a realization.

Her Father; had said the same thing to her as I did.

We all knew Patty; later we all knew Patrick. None of us;

'Ever' had the chance to really get to know, Pat!

These clannish people kept 'him' away from us.

Patrick was 'our flesh and blood;' he did not 'belong to them.'

I wonder in the six hours; he laid their fighting for his life; did My Son realize; "He; was not 'one of them?'

In Patrick's first baby picture; he looked liked he was making 'fists.'

We teased him through the years about being born ready to 'fight.'

In the State Police Report; I read about the accident; The State Trooper stated; "I gave him two breaths of air; stood back and watched." With his left hand, he began to make what appeared to be 'a fist?'

CHAPTER 31

SHOOTING STAR

During the long winter months in the northwoods; My Neighbor and Best Friend gave me a 'special paper.'

I read the paper and donated the money.

In the northern Part of Michigan; before the Mackinac Bridge; which connects the two peninsulas of Michigan; there is a very large "Cross in the Woods."

I donated money in memory of Patrick.

In the summer of 2002; a new walkway to the "Cross" will be created.

One of the large paver stones will have My Son's name on it.

Under his name in parenthesis shall be the words "SHOOTING STAR."

In my new area; My Brother took me to a garden nursery.

We went in two different directions; both looking at plants.

I called My Brother's name and he came to my side.

I said "Look, at the name of this plant."

He did and 'our' eyes caught each others!

The name of the beautiful plant was "SHOOTING STAR."

Aurora Borealis

It is thriving in my front porch and with a Mother's Loving Touch; I "Baby" it!

About the Author

Due to the serious nature of my book, I have to remain anonymous. This decision was made for reasons of privacy and safety. As you read my book this will become clearer to you!

Printed in the United States
1503700001B/17